About This Book

The Irish high crosses are the most original and interesting of all the monuments which stud the Irish landscape. They are of international importance in early medieval art. For their period there is little to equal them in the sculpture of Western Europe as a whole.

This book gives basic information about the crosses. A general survey is followed by an inventory to accompany the large collection of photographs which illustrate their variety and richness. In this way readers will readily have at their disposal an extensive range of the images created in stone by sculptors working in Ireland over a thousand years ago.

In the composition of this book the text and drawings have been the responsibility of Hilary Richardson and John Scarry has been responsible for the photographs from the Photographic Collection of the Office of Public Works, Ireland, which make up the major bulk of the illustrations.

HILARY RICHARDSON teaches in the Department of Archaeology, University College Dublin, and has lectured on Irish crosses at international conferences in Armenia, Georgia, Austria and Italy to which she was invited. In 1985 she was awarded the first exchange fellowship between the Royal Irish Academy and the Soviet Academy of Sciences, and carried out research in Georgia and Armenia; while there she gave an interview on Armenian television about Irish crosses. Educated at Girton College, Cambridge, she graduated in Archaeology and Anthropology under scholars such as Nora Chadwick, Glyn Daniel, Rachel Bromwich and Peter Hunter Blair. She has qualifications in art, having studied in Dublin and abroad, and an MA in History of Art from UCD, where she studied with Dr Françoise Henry.

JOHN SCARRY has worked for many years in the photographic section of the National Monuments Branch, Office of Public Works. His work has made him familiar with all the various types of monuments including high crosses which he feels that up until now have not received the same amount of public attention as other aspects of Ireland's heritage.

An Introduction to
IRISH HIGH CROSSES

Frontispiece: Last Judgement, Cross of Muiredach, Monasterboice.

An Introduction to
IRISH HIGH CROSSES

HILARY RICHARDSON & JOHN SCARRY

MERCIER PRESS

MERCIER PRESS

© Hilary Richardson & John Scarry, 1990

A CIP record is available for this book from the British Library.

ISBN 0 85342 954 5

Design: Joseph Gervin
Typesetting: Typeform Ltd.

10 9 8 7

**To Niko Chubinashvili
eminent art historian and authority
on early Georgian carving in wood and stone,
this book is dedicated with great respect
and gratitude for his unstinted help
and encouragement**

Printed in Ireland by Colour Books Ltd.

Contents

Map   6

Preface   7

Acknowledgements   8

Introduction   9

1   **The Cross**   11

2   **Structure**   12

3   **Stone Carving in Ireland**   14

4   **The Siting of Crosses**   15

5   **Inscriptions**   16

6   **Development of Crosses**   17

    Ahenny or Ossory Group

    Transitional Crosses

    Scripture Crosses

    Late Crosses

7   **Interpretation of the Crosses**   21

    The Triumph of the Cross

    The Origin of the Ring

    Links with Jerusalem

8   **Past Study on the Irish Crosses**   27

9   **Catalogue of Crosses and Illustrations**   29

    List of Plates   51

    Bibliography   151

MONUMENT SITES

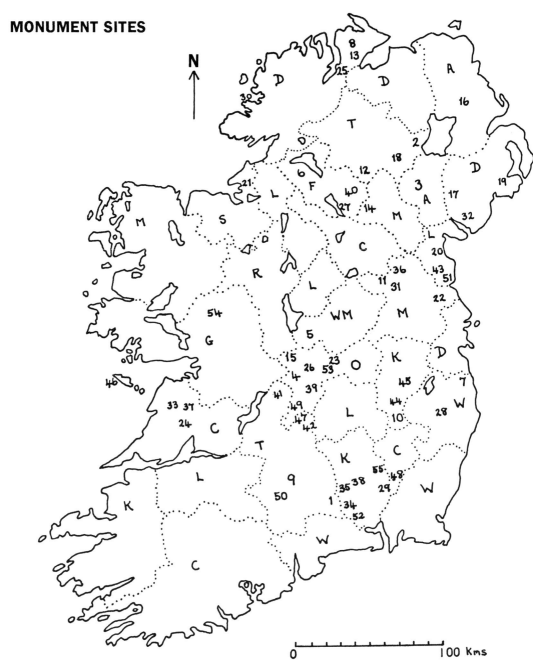

1	Ahenny	15	Clonmacnois	29	Graiguenamanagh	43	Monasterboice
2	Arboe	16	Connor	30	Inishkeel	44	Moone
3	Armagh	17	Donaghmore, Down	31	Kells (Co. Meath)	45	Old Kilcullen
4	Banagher	18	Donaghmore, Tyrone	32	Kilbroney	46	Onaght
5	Bealin	19	Downpatrick	33	Kilfenora	47	Roscrea
6	Boho	20	Dromiskin	34	Kilkieran	48	St Mullins
7	Bray	21	Drumcliff	35	Killamery	49	Seir Kieran
8	Carndonagh	22	Duleek	36	Killary	50	Templeneiry
9	Cashel	23	Durrow	37	Kilnaboy	51	Termonfeckin
10	Castledermot	24	Dysert O'Dea	38	Kilree	52	Tibberaghny
11	Castlekieran	25	Fahan Mura	39	Kinnitty	53	Tihilly
12	Clogher	26	Gallen Priory	40	Lisnaskea	54	Tuam
13	Clonca	27	Galloon	41	Lorrha	55	Ullard
14	Clones	28	Glendalough	42	Mona Incha		

Preface

'It was a stone cross with a circle ... The crowned figure in the centre was still whole; panel above panel, back, front and sides, showed crowds of figures in relief.

'Or were they figures and patterns encrusted on stone that had long been sunken in the sea? They were as worn as the words in prayers the people said. But examining the panels one began to find meaning in the figures and to understand what was significant in the whole monument.

'It stood at its right height, a cross with a wide circle round its arms, the crowned and dying figure in the centre, and that circle of stone, and the panels, front and sides, filled with figures. A cross has not a monumental shape: straight up and straight across it lacks fullness and solidarity. But the sculptor of a thousand years ago, by encircling the arms, made the cross of stone massive, a solid. The one who did this had lived in this place, seeing the stones upon the hill (known then for a kingly tomb), hearing the cawing of the rooks, seeing these lithe young men with their mountain ponies, seeing the beggar woman with her tangled hair and dusty feet as the straggler after some defeat.

'All the folk today could be set along the sides of the cross, enhancing the significance of the figure in the centre – the man, his wife and child in their cart; the ballad-singer; the man driving pigs. And the circle conveyed that idea of return which was in the minds of the people here of a thousand years ago . . . ' *

*Adapted from 'Pilgrimage Home' by Padraic Colum (Sanford Sternlicht, editor, *Selected Short Stories of Padraic Colum,* Syracuse University Press, 1985, pp. 78–80. By permission of the publisher.)

Acknowledgements

We have pleasure in thanking the following public bodies for permission to reproduce photographs: the Office of Public Works in Ireland, the Department of the Environment for Northern Ireland, and the National Library, Vienna. Individual thanks are due to I. Crozier, Ann Hamlin, M. Herity, A. Hintze and R. Kenia for photographs in the Photographic Archives of the Department of Archaeology, UCD, established by Dr Françoise Henry. We are most grateful to Elinor Wiltshire for photographs, and in addition Hilary Richardson is greatly indebted to her for constant help and encouragement over many years. The generosity of Domhnall Ó Murchadha must also be mentioned in sharing his vast store of knowledge about the crosses. Grateful thanks are also due to Mary Feehan of the Mercier Press.

Photo credits:
Department of the Environment for Northern Ireland for nos. 7, 9, 16, 17, 18, 19, 20, 21,22, 71, 72 73,74, 75, 76, 99, 100, 101.
H.S. Crawford for nos. 6, 15, 27, 69, 70, 128, 174, 196, 199.
I. Crozier for no. 68.
A. Hamlin for nos. 47, 48.
F. Henry for nos. 8, 44, 45, 46, 95, 97, 127, 172, 173, II.
M. Herity for no. I.
A. Hintze for nos. 14, 134, 171, 183.
R. Kenia, for no. IX.
H. Richardson for nos. 5, 67, 143, 144, VI.
Vienna, National Library for no. VIII.
E. Wiltshire for nos. 11, 31, 32, 33, 42, 49, 50, 62, 66, 92, 93, 96, 98, 109, 157, 168, 180, III, IV.
All the photographs otherwise are courtesy of the Office of Public Works, Dublin; no. 90 is from the Wiltshire Collection, Office of Public Works.

Introduction

The high crosses are the most arresting and attractive of all the monuments which stud the Irish countryside. They are the most typically Irish. Indeed the very shape of the Celtic or ringed cross, silhouetted against the sky, has come to be identified with Ireland.

The aim of this book is to illustrate the major crosses. It is not intended to be a complete catalogue including every carving of note. That would be a task well beyond the scope of a small practical survey. Instead within more modest dimensions it is proposed to give a comprehensive view or panorama of the crosses. It is hoped to cover their salient features and individual characteristics. In each case the sides of the chief monuments are shown by a selection of photographs. Seeing them grouped together gives some idea of the wealth of stone-carving in Ireland in early medieval times. There is ornament in abundance and lively figure scenes. The subtle diversity of the proportions of ring to upright, of breadth to height can be observed, along with the presence of individual schools of sculpture or even, in one or two places, the hand of a master sculptor.

There are in existence many excellent studies on the crosses written by scholars over the years. Generally their choice of illustrations is made for various and particular reasons so that certain aspects of a cross become quite familiar through their pages. Other aspects may not appear however.

It may be hard for the interested reader to find an all round representation of a given monument. Frequently for instance the north side is neglected because the lighting tends to be poor. The pictures assembled in the present collection may fill the gap to some extent. The impact of the shapes is striking, while the detail of the panels of biblical subjects needs careful inspection. The high crosses are at their most impressive when they are allowed to speak for themselves.

Impressive the crosses certainly are. It is true to say that their colossal stature, figuratively speaking, amongst contemporary carvings is not properly recognised or appreciated. As works of international importance they have been sadly neglected. Their location, rather off the beaten track of the visual high spots of European art, has been against them. So it is necessary to point out that the Irish high crosses are unique documents in the history of sculpture. Carved at a time in western Europe when there was little opportunity either to commission or produce work of a monumental character, they stand unrivalled in stone in the grandeur of their conception and execution. For their period there is nothing on a comparable scale elsewhere this side of Byzantium, except for the carvings of Britain. A multitude of fragments shows what must have once existed in England. In Ireland though, the high crosses have remained a living part of the landscape. Their survival has been astonishing. A few suffered badly, witness the scarred remnants at Connor, Co. Antrim, or Armagh, but it is fortunate how much remains from that remote period when Christianity was the chief driving force behind patronage of the arts.

The crosses of Ireland and Britain are practically the only elaborate free-standing monuments of the early Middle Ages in all the west of Europe. Following the disintegration of the Roman Empire there was a lack of monumental work on any large scale. There was no place for it in the so-called Dark Ages, in a situation of continuous wars and upheavals with the spread and eventual settlement of the barbarian tribes. Few monuments belonging to the period prior to the eleventh century have come down to us. Confined to the British Isles and Ireland the crosses share a common theme, though each region has well defined characteristics. In Britain they are found mainly in the north of England, in Wales, in Cornwall and some parts of Scotland. There is no clear understanding at present of how the different groups relate to one another. The Irish high crosses form an outstanding, distinctive series of their own which must be considered independently while not forgetting links with neighbouring carvings. A group of crosses on Iona and the adjoining area of western Scotland are in the Irish tradition. The monastery at Iona had been founded by St Colmcille in 563, when he left Ireland, and it became a focus of activity for Celtic Christianity in the following centuries. These crosses, some of which are ringed in the Irish style, fit within the same background as the Irish high crosses.

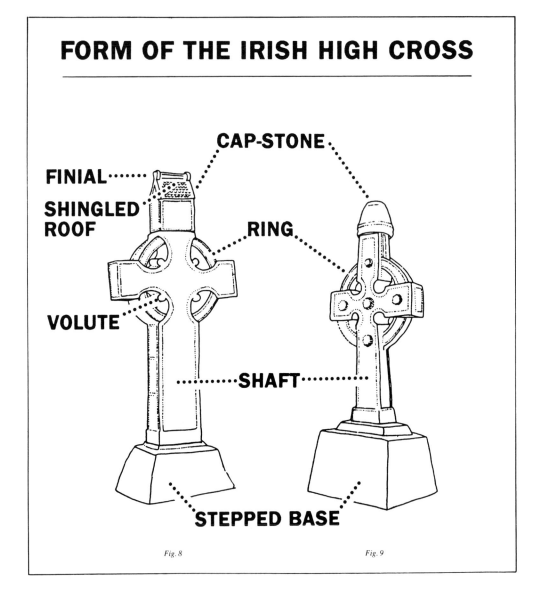

FORM OF THE IRISH HIGH CROSS

CAP-STONE

FINIAL

SHINGLED ROOF

RING

VOLUTE

SHAFT

STEPPED BASE

Fig. 8   *Fig. 9*

The Cross

It is a mistake to think of a high cross as representing the Crucifixion. The Irish crosses seldom bear figures in high relief and only the latest examples have an image of the Crucifixion in the round. The shape of the cross stands not merely as the instrument of Christ's punishment, but is actually the embodiment and symbol of Christ. In Christian iconography the cross is Christ in person.

The Irish crosses belong to a period stretching from the seventh to the twelfth centuries. In the earliest Christian art the Crucifixion was not depicted. The shame and ignominy associated with it made it for many years an unsuitable subject for portrayal. As a means of execution it remained in force until it was abolished by the Emperor Constantine. He became the champion of Christianity in the first part of the fourth century and is thought to have introduced the use of the Chi-Rho monogram, the special sign symbolising the Christian faith. Here the first two letters in Greek (Ch and R) of Christ's name are combined together in a number of ways, often enclosed within a circle or a victor's laurel wreath *(fig. 1, fig. 2–7 below)*.

Fig. 1

Chi and Rho, first two letters of Christ's name in Greek

Historically the cult of the cross burst into life from the time of Constantine. Christians began to display their beliefs visually and make open confirmation of their now legal religion since they were no longer afraid of persecution. The cross predominated above every other Christian emblem.

The source of many of the ideas underlying the form and content of the high crosses goes back to this early period of Christian art. In the intervening centuries a whole new stratification of religious thought and tradition has overlaid the beliefs which were once widespread at the beginning of the Christian era. So it happens that the original intention behind the work of early artists and sculptors has often been forgotten. New ways of thinking have altered perception year after year, through the growth of theology, new Church dogmas and social change. It is rather difficult for us in the twentieth century to shake off the massive accretions which have accumulated down the ages and to start again with a reasonably fresh eye.

After a brief consideration of facts about the crosses, we shall return again to the question of the interpretation of the high crosses and the symbolism they express.

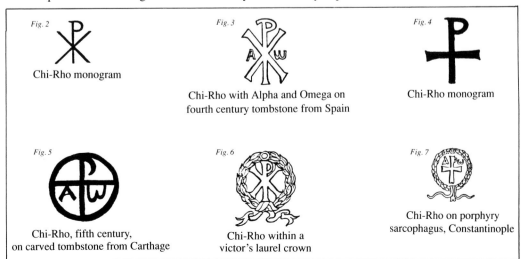

Fig. 2 — Chi-Rho monogram

Fig. 3 — Chi-Rho with Alpha and Omega on fourth century tombstone from Spain

Fig. 4 — Chi-Rho monogram

Fig. 5 — Chi-Rho, fifth century, on carved tombstone from Carthage

Fig. 6 — Chi-Rho within a victor's laurel crown

Fig. 7 — Chi-Rho on porphyry sarcophagus, Constantinople

Structure

A high cross may be described as a big, square pillar of stone terminating at the top in the shape of a cross. It is carved on its four sides with carvings in low relief, often arranged in panels. It is set in a base of cubic or pyramid form, sometimes fashioned in a series of steps. The height varies from about three metres to four and a half metres or even six metres in a few cases.

Normally a cross consists of three elements: a separate base, a shaft usually in one with the ring, and a cap-stone *(figs. 8–9)*.

It may be built from several blocks of stone but there is no hard and fast rule. Bases frequently survive on their own. Some tall shafts are in segments, while occasionally a crosshead is mounted on a shaft above a special ornamental band which resembles a capital on top of a pillar, crowned by a cross *(see plate 14)*. Tenons and mortices are used to unite the different sections. Usually cap-stones are carved from separate blocks, though some of the finest crosses are monolithic. The cap-stone is an integral part of the design, completing the image the sculptor had of the cross in its entirety *(fig. 10, 11, 12)*.

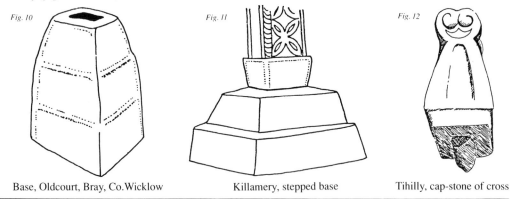

| *Fig. 10* | *Fig. 11* | *Fig. 12* |
| Base, Oldcourt, Bray, Co.Wicklow | Killamery, stepped base | Tihilly, cap-stone of cross |

A ring of stone connecting the arms to the upright creates the characteristic outline of the wheeled or Celtic cross. In Ireland there are altogether just under three hundred crosses or the remains of crosses, and many of these are plain without a ring. However a recent study shows that sixty-eight crosses have the typical open ring, and almost as many have a solid circle of stone.[1] A number of different explanations for the origin of the ring have been put forward, some symbolic, some functional. Whatever the reason for the shape, the Celtic cross demonstrates the tendency of Irish artists always to work within their own idiom.

A final feature may be remarked which occurs on ninth and tenth century crosses. These are four stone discs or volutes inserted in the frame of the crosshead, either adorning the inner surface of each quadrant of the ring or at the central junction.

The stone most generally used is sandstone. Sometimes the weather has taken its toll and fine detail has been worn away. A contrast in the rate of erosion can be seen even on the same monument, like the West Cross at Monasterboice where two stones of differing quality appear to have been chosen, one for the head and one for the rest of the cross. Granite is the material used for the crosses in the valley of the River Barrow, in the neighbourhood of the Leinster mountains. The crosses of the Midlands are often of gritstone, while in Co. Clare crosses are carved from the native blue-grey limestone. However the colour of the stone in all probability did not matter as paint could have been used to pick out the decoration. Carved panels of interlacing ribbons, painted in contrasting colours, would have been comparable to pages in contemporary illuminated manuscripts.

FINIALS   SHINGLED ROOF

ANTAE

Fig. 13

Solomon's Temple from The Temptation of Christ, *Book of Kells*, f.202 v

Plate 1:   St Martin's Cross, Iona (a and b)

There is evidence that additional pieces were fixed to certain crosses. There are short stone projections on either side of the Fahan Mura slab *(see plates 93–95)*, while St Martin's Cross, Iona, has vertical slots in its short arms *(plate 1)*. Wooden components may have been added. It is possible that the double mouldings found on the tapered narrow sides of some of the Ahenny group were functional, perhaps fitting hollows in wooden side pieces. Again, empty circular settings in St John's Cross, Iona, must originally have been intended to hold large bosses, possibly of metal. A massive wooden boss, carved with interlace, was found in the recent excavations of Viking Dublin. Features of wooden construction can sometimes be observed, petrified in stone. Good examples are the carved finials at the ends of the ridge pole of the small houses or oratories which form the cap-stones of many crosses. In a wooden building the crossed beams projected above the line of the roof and could be treated decoratively as finials. They are drawn in the *Book of Kells'* illustration of the Temple of Solomon at Jerusalem *(Fig. 13)*, and occur on most of the metal-cased house-shaped shrines also. On the high crosses the finials have lost all practical significance as they are small models in stone of a wooden construction.

Stone Carving in Ireland

There was no native tradition of building in stone or the use of cut stone in Ireland, though monumental art did exist in prehistoric times with the setting up of standing stones. When the first free-standing ringed crosses appeared in the eighth century they represented an entirely new aspect of Irish art. The high crosses are complex works, carefully measured and organised in three dimensions. Prehistoric monuments and early cross-inscribed pillars did not change the natural shape of the stone, and carving was usually confined to surface decoration. The first free- standing cross seems to be at Carndonagh *(see plates 28–31)* in the far north-west in Co. Donegal, with Fahan Mura *(see plates 93–95)* nearby, where the large upright slab in the graveyard bears the only early inscription in Greek in Ireland and has on either face skilfully carved crosses in low relief, woven from broad ribbons of stone in the same style as the interlace in the *Book of Durrow (circa 650)*. These are best dated to the mid seventh century. There is no absolute dating for many of the stone carvings around the countryside. However the type of site on which slabs and cross-stones occur often indicates an early date. They were set up around early monasteries, perhaps where no remains of buildings exist now or just a few ruins. A large proportion are found along the west coast or on islands which were suitable places for retreat or for hermitages *(plate II)*. The crosses carved or engraved on pillars are of a wide variety: sometimes a Greek cross inscribed in a circle, or a Latin cross with wedge shaped terminals, or with the arms curling into spirals *(fig. 14)*. Recumbent grave slabs survive in large numbers at some important monasteries, such as Clonmacnois. Their pleasing cross designs are matched by engraved inscriptions in beautiful lettering *(plate III)*.

Plate II: Crucifixion slab, Duvillaun

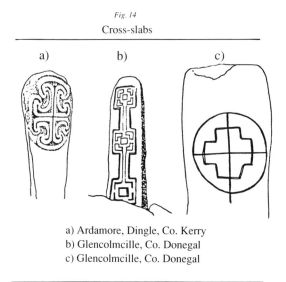

Fig. 14

Cross-slabs

a)   b)   c)

a) Ardamore, Dingle, Co. Kerry
b) Glencolmcille, Co. Donegal
c) Glencolmcille, Co. Donegal

The names of the deceased, recorded in these short formal prayers, can be identified with entries in the *Annals* from the early eighth century. The high cross, on the other hand, is never a funerary memorial so far as we know. It is clearly a separate conception, unrelated to the other stone monuments and unique in its own right.

The Siting of Crosses

High crosses were erected in the precincts of monasteries where they had a protective significance and probably served as points of assembly for religious ceremonies. Recent research on the choice of biblical scenes in their carved panels suggests that in some cases they had a special place in the liturgy of the early Church. Others were termon crosses which marked a boundary *(see plate 43)*. In addition the votive character of some crosses is borne out by inscriptions. The south cross at Kells, Co. Meath, is called the 'Cross of Patrick and Columba' in its inscription on the base *(see plate 114)*. A diagram in the eighth century *Book of Mulling* shows a plan of the monastery with its circular enclosure *(fig. 15)*.

A number of crosses, dedicated to the prophets and evangelists, are marked outside the ramparts, while other named crosses are situated within the sanctuary.

It is known that Iona once possessed many crosses, and names are preserved for St Martin's Cross and St John's Cross among those that remain. The general rule for the orientation of crosses is east-west.

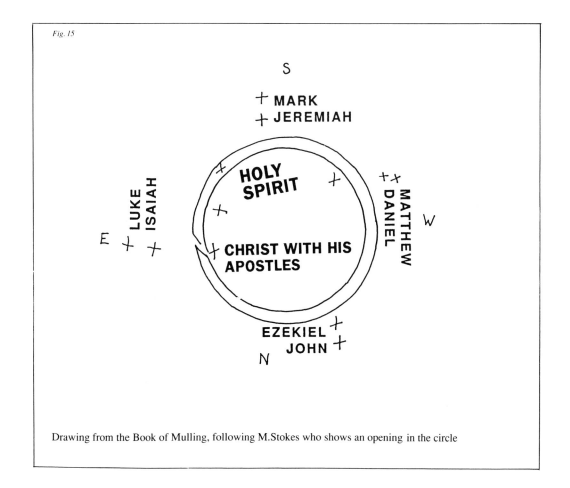

Fig. 15

Drawing from the Book of Mulling, following M.Stokes who shows an opening in the circle

Inscriptions

As a result of new work on inscriptions considerable advance has been made in the dating of the high crosses in recent years. The chronology of a number of crosses is reasonably secure. There are more inscriptions extant than had been recognised. Many crosses were designed with a plain panel at the bottom of the shaft to take lettering. However, in the case of the Cross of Muiredach at Monasterboice *(see plate 157)*, the finest of all the scripture crosses, it seems that the inscription was added as an afterthought because it weaves behind the sculptured cats, carved almost in the round, on the foot of the shaft. This cross was erected in the early tenth century by the abbot of Monasterboice who died in 923. It belongs to the same workshop as the Cross of the Scriptures erected at Clonmacnois for Flann Sinna, King of Ireland, in the first years of the tenth century *(see plates 63–66)*. The cross at Kinnitty, Co. Offaly, was put up by Flann's father, Máelsechnaill mac Máelruanaid, who reigned from 846–862 *(see plates 129–131)*. From rubbings it has been possible to read inscriptions on both the broad faces. One side in translation reads:– 'A prayer for King Máelsechnaill son of Máelruanaid. A prayer for the King of Ireland.' Máelsechnaill established himself as King of all Ireland in 859.

A good measure of wealth is reflected in the magnificence of the crosses. Patronage of vision and substance was necessary. The crosses were commissioned by kings and abbots, just as the luxury Gospel books bear evidence of the prosperity of the monasteries in whose scriptoria they were illuminated.

Plate III: Clonmacnois grave-slab, O̅R̅ DO DAINÉIL

Development of the Crosses

The crosses fall into several broad groups according to location and style. A loose chronology has been generally accepted for them although it needs to be more securely established. The difficulty of dating stone monuments has already been noted. A reasonable framework for the crosses emerges through the dates given by inscriptions and also through parallels in ornament in work in other fields such as metalwork and manuscript illumination.

The appearance of the crosses develops in four rough stages. The earliest ringed crosses relied on abstract decoration to a large extent with designs in interlacing and fret patterns covering the main surfaces. Then biblical scenes were introduced more prominently, rather tentatively at first. A mixture of ornament and figure subjects marks an intermediary stage before the remarkable change to figured scenes in panels, found on the scripture crosses. Finally a late group of crosses have single figures, usually of Christ or a bishop, in very bold relief on the upper part.

The Ahenny or Ossory Group

The earliest group, of which the North Cross at Ahenny *(see plates 1–6)* is a fine example, probably dates from the eighth to ninth centuries and is found in a restricted location, only a few miles apart, in Co. Tipperary and Co. Kilkenny. The Ahenny crosses are extraordinary in one way, in that although carved in stone they imitate wooden crosses encased in metal plates. The hatched mouldings around the sides copy a metal binding which would cover the edges of sheets of metal; while the large decorated bosses imitate enamelled studs superimposed above rivets which would hold the metal plates together. The stone bosses here have no practical function at all. They sometimes seem to attach the ring to the cross-arms and upright, giving the illusion that they are practical. The cross itself is mainly devoted to ornament with designs found in contemporary metalwork. Some patterns clearly resemble work in enamel while others copy the slanting facets of work in gilt chipcarving, a technique borrowed from the Anglo-Saxons and used by Irish craftsmen to enhance the play of light and shade in cast metal.

It is plain to see that the Ahenny crosses are reflecting in stone the magnificence of jewelled crosses made from precious metals, gold or silver, encrusted with gems, pearls and enamels. A great deal of effort and skill was expended on the rather strange task of reproducing the work of the jeweller and metalsmith in the unlikely medium of stone, and we can be sure it was done for a compelling reason. Every angle of the cross has been planned. Even the outer sides of the ring are divided in opposing planes to catch the light. Of all the crosses, these are the most three-dimensional.

Transitional Crosses

A change in the balance between ornament and figure carving on the crosses is contemporary with the Céli Dé or Culdee movement and may have been due to its influence. It was a time of spiritual reform with a new emphasis on the religious life and asceticism. Biblical subjects become increasingly important. The network of spirals, interlacings and fret patterns on the crosses at Ahenny, Kilkieran, Kilree and Killamery gives way to figured scenes on the main surfaces of the cross. Ornament persists but is relegated to panels on the narrow sides or less prominent areas.

Two crosses seem to mark a transition towards the panelled organisation of the scripture crosses. These are the South Cross at Clonmacnois *(see plates 59–62)* and the Cross of Patrick and Columba at Kells *(see plates 111–114)*. It is interesting that both these crosses have connections with Iona. The South Cross at Clonmacnois bears a strong resemblance to the Ahenny group but it also has a representation of the Crucifixion on the west face. The ornamental bosses stand out in bold relief and are now semispherical. This is the striking treatment found on the Iona crosses, where the entire east face of St Martin's Cross *(see plate 1)* is an interlocking orchestration of raised bosses and serpents. The Cross of Patrick and Columba at Kells, although rather small in size, has an attraction of its own with subjects freely rendered and full of movement. It appears to date to the first Viking raids on Iona, with the exodus of the monks to Kells early in the ninth century. Alone of all the crosses it shares the same concern for the symbols of the Evangelists that is so significant in the *Book of Kells,* where the calf, the lion, the eagle and the man are portrayed at every opportunity *(fig. 16).*

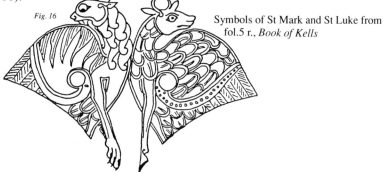

Fig. 16

Symbols of St Mark and St Luke from fol.5 r., *Book of Kells*

Scripture Crosses

A group of about thirty crosses, widely scattered from the far north to Co. Carlow, are heavily panelled with figure carvings. These are sometimes known as scripture crosses after the *Cross na screaptra,* the Cross of the Scriptures at Clonmacnois *(see plates 63–66),* mentioned in the *Annals* in 1060. They may be dated between the ninth and first part of the tenth century, and show a transformation in Irish sculpture. For the first time Irish artists departed from the traditional vision of the Celts. Now they chose to depict narrative subjects, realistically represented. Perhaps the historical situation with the need to assert Christian values in the face of the Viking incursions may explain this change. The new style of figure carving in relief must have had some model. In all probability there was contact with Carolingian work, where ivory book covers portray similar biblical scenes.

The iconography of the biblical subjects on the crosses is of great interest. They go back to the earliest cycles of Christian art. There is repetition of a fairly limited range of themes from both Old and New Testaments, and also episodes depicting the first Christian hermits in the desert, St Paul and St Anthony, who were the founders of monasticism. The biblical scenes have symbolic reference to salvation and the Eucharist. They continue a programme found in the earliest art in the catacombs and on sculptured sarcophagi. Emphasis is on the 'Help of God' in adversity: subjects such as Daniel in the Lions' Den or Noah, which were originally used in Jewish prayers. To these subjects were added further Old Testament scenes *(fig. 17)* which prefigure the life of Christ and scenes from the New Testament, especially miracles.

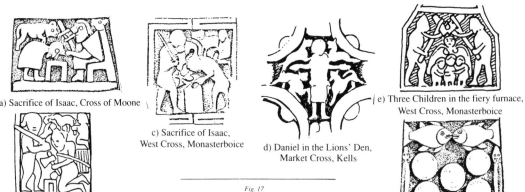

a) Sacrifice of Isaac, Cross of Moone

b) Sacrifice of Isaac, Cross of Durrow

c) Sacrifice of Isaac, West Cross, Monasterboice

d) Daniel in the Lions' Den, Market Cross, Kells

e) Three Children in the fiery furnace, West Cross, Monasterboice

f) Multiplication of the loaves and fishes, Cross of Moone

Fig. 17
Biblical scenes from the crosses

Irish poems and hymns of the early ninth century, such as the hymn of St Colmán moccu Chlúasaig, follow the same formula. In addition recent research suggests that for practical use the carvings could be attuned to the seasons of the liturgical year. Certain scenes relate to historical personages. Even mythological explanations have been offered in some cases. Enigmatic hunting scenes or processions of horsemen still occur as they did on the earlier crosses. Many scenes are of uncertain meaning, with a number of possible interpretations.

On the Scripture crosses the Last Judgement usually occupies one side of the crosshead, with the Crucifixion on the other face. The Second Coming of Christ was a major idea in medieval thought. At Monasterboice on the Cross of Muiredach the depiction of the Last Judgement is spread over the entire sweep of the eastern face of the crosshead and cannot fail to impress the spectator *(see plate 159 and Frontispiece)*.

Yet although the figure carving at Monasterboice is naturalistic, the abstract character of Celtic work can still be felt. Françoise Henry noted that the Cross of Muiredach seemed to be composed on the theme of the semispherical spiral. Such spirals are used to decorate the ring and also the side panels, and from a distance they seem to cover the two arms of the cross. But on examination this 'ornament' is discovered to be the Blessed and the Damned on either side of the judgement throne. It is remarkable that the Last Judgement here, with St Michael weighing the souls, was carved soon after 900, some two centuries before the same scene filled the tympana of Romanesque churches on the continent.

Late Crosses
The figurative art comes to an end very suddenly. The crosses of the eleventh and first half of the twelfth centuries are quite different. They make for diversity, from St Patrick's Cross at Cashel with pillar-like supports at either side, the imposing cross at Dysert O'Dea and other crosses of Co. Clare, carved from the local grey limestone *(fig. 18)*, and the large Tuam cross, erected by King Turlough O'Connor (1106–1156).

Fig. 18

Large cross in Kilfenora churchyard, east face

These now show archaic tendencies and ornament again takes a prominent place. Spirals have begun to disappear whilst animal interlacings with strong Scandinavian features predominate, for contact with the Vikings had left its mark. On one side of these crosses there is always a representation of the Crucifixion in very bold relief.

The series comes to an end in the twelfth century with the coming of the Normans, and later medieval crosses are rather different.

To sum up the development of the crosses, it appears in the first place that it was the shape of the cross itself which was all important. The early ornamental crosses raised the outline of the cross, ringed in stone, against the sky. Later, as time went on, an elaborate theological commentary was spread in panels of biblical scenes over the surface of the monument. The scripture crosses are characterised by clearly defined legible scenes of narrative figure carving. The biblical stories are depicted in detail so that people could learn their message easily; they have been called 'sermons in stones'. Lastly, in a final phase the cross becomes a huge crucifix.

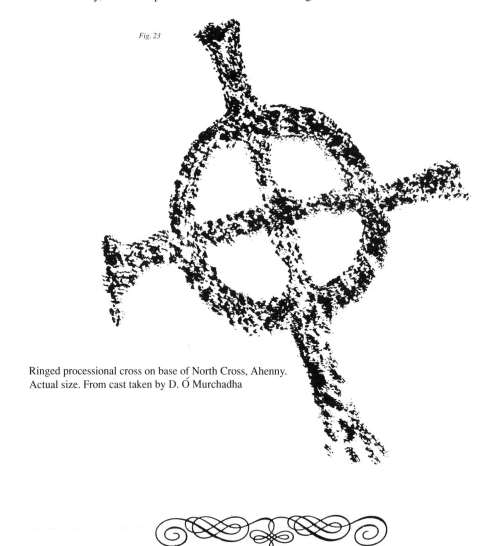

Fig. 23

Ringed processional cross on base of North Cross, Ahenny.
Actual size. From cast taken by D. Ó Murchadha

Interpretation of the Crosses

There can be no doubt that the figuration of the cross itself was the fundamental reason for building these monuments. An examination of the ornament or of the iconography of the carved scenes tends to obscure this fact, which is basic to their existence. However a great deal of work remains to be done on all aspects of the crosses and in particular we lack a complete understanding of the purpose and background underlying their erection. Information about sculptors and artisans in early medieval Ireland is meagre at present. Further research in written sources, such as law tracts, may throw light on many unanswered questions.

The Triumph of the Cross
A number of the ideas behind the setting up of the High Crosses in Ireland go back ultimately to the time of Constantine the Great. There were major changes for Christians at this period. From Constantine onwards for several centuries the cross was used principally as a sign of triumph, of the victory of Christ and of the Christian faith.

The Feast of the Exaltation of the Cross became an important festival in the Church. Although the Irish crosses are exceptional in western Europe, they have close parallels in the East Christian world, especially in Armenia and Georgia. Here stone monuments topped by a cross were set up in considerable numbers between the fifth and seventh centuries. Extensive fragments survive *(fig. 19)*.

Fig. 19

a)

b)

a) Small base carved with a cross, sixth century, Bolnisi, Georgia

b) Part of shaft showing Sacrifice of Isaac, seventh century, Garnahovit, Armenia

They usually consist of a cubic base with a shaft of rectangular section. Some are divided in panels to depict biblical subjects similar to those that appear on the Irish crosses *(plates IV, V, VI)*. In Armenia these monuments cease with the Arab conquest. The Armenian khatchkar or cross-stone evolves from the ninth century onwards, replacing the earlier cross-topped pillars. It is a slab, mounted on a plinth, with an elaborate cross motif decorating its front, west-facing surface. The khatchkar is the typical Armenian monument, indeed an emblem of Armenia itself *(plate VII)*. But from the very beginning of Christianity in these parts crosses were set up to announce the triumph of the faith. The first evangelist in Armenia, St Gregory the Illuminator, had crosses put up; while in Georgia St Nino's wooden cross is famous, celebrating the conversion of Georgia to Christianity in the first part of the fourth century. The site above Mtskheta where her cross was erected was used two centuries later for the building of Djvari or Church of the Holy Cross, a place of pilgrimage of prime importance still for the Georgian Orthodox Church.

Some of the features of the late classical world of Constantine have left their mark on the Irish crosses. In the first place the tradition of free-standing monuments to commemorate an event, such as a general's success in battle, was common in Roman times. Many well known examples of triumphal columns remain. A tall stone pillar or obelisk was set on a cubic base. In a Christian context like the early monuments in the Caucasus, a cross surmounted the pillar to signify the triumph of Christ *(fig. 20)*.

Plate V: Brdadzor, tall stele, sixth century

Plate VI: Odzun, south pillar from east, sixth century

Plate IV: Stele from Haridj, sixth century

Plate VII: Khatchkar, 1184, at Sanahin

Constantine's own conversion followed the vision he had before the Battle of the Milvian Bridge in 312. He recounted the story to his biographer, Eusebius, bishop of Caesarea. In advance of the battle Constantine prayed for help and 'a most marvellous sign appeared to him from heaven. He said that about noon he saw with his own eyes a cross of light in the heavens, above the sun, and bearing this inscription "by this sign shalt thou conquer".' Having won the battle Constantine built a triumphal arch in Rome in 315 to celebrate the victory.

The origin of the ring

A triumph was an occasion of great rejoicing in the Roman army. Having won a battle the Roman general's standard was erected outside his tent, bearing his shield and victor's laurel wreath (*fig. 21*). It was also carried before him in procession.

The victor's wreath or garland of laurel is considered by some scholars to be the origin of the ring on the high crosses. In the *Life of Constantine* it tells how Constantine, directed by his vision, ordered the Chi-Rho monogram to be placed within a wreath at the top of the imperial standard. Thus the triumph of Christ was proclaimed (*fig. 22*).

A Chi-Rho or equal armed cross enclosed within a circle is a frequent motif in early art. In this form the cross is inside the circle, whereas the arms of the typical Irish cross pierce the ring. One solution is that the ring is actually a halo around the cross which represents Christ. Many other theories about the origin of the ring have been put forward. A functional view maintains that the ring came from a wooden prototype, where diagonal braces strengthened the cross and in turn these were changed from straight pieces into the curves of a circle for aesthetic reasons.[2] On the other hand connections with prehistoric sun symbolism cannot be ignored. In lines of early Irish poetry Christ is sometimes addressed as the sun. An example comes from a metrical litany of the Virgin Mary:–

> *A rigdorais rogaidhe triasar chin i cri*
> *Grien taithnemhach togaide, Isu mac De bii*
> *O royal door elect, through which came into the body*
> *The shining choice Sun, Jesus, Son of the living God.*[3]

There is no doubt that the ringed cross was favoured in Ireland at an early date. It is engraved on many Irish grave slabs, mainly of the ninth century. One dating from as early as 720 at Clonmacnois is identified by the name in the *Annals*.[4] Evidence of a ringed processional cross can be seen on the base of the North Cross at Ahenny. It is carried by the cleric leading the funeral cortège (*fig. 23*).

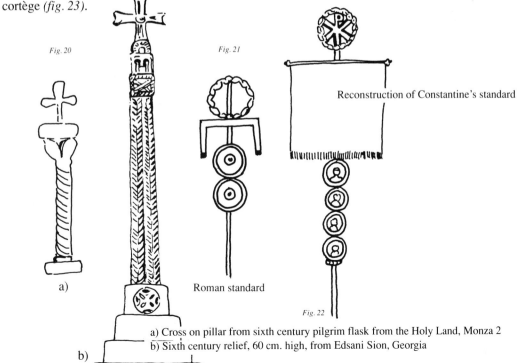

Fig. 20

Fig. 21

Reconstruction of Constantine's standard

a)

Roman standard

b)

Fig. 22

a) Cross on pillar from sixth century pilgrim flask from the Holy Land, Monza 2
b) Sixth century relief, 60 cm. high, from Edsani Sion, Georgia

An early reference dating to near 800 also should be mentioned. A short treatise on the mass in old Irish is included in the *Stowe Missal,* now in the Royal Irish Academy. It speaks of the circle-wheel as part of a cross. Instructions are given for the division of the bread, set in the form of a cross. There are to be twenty particles in its circle-wheel *(cuairtroth)* for the confraction at Easter and Christmas.[5] Clearly the ringed cross was thought of as the norm in Ireland. It is hard to explain why the extension of the arms beyond the circle rarely occurs elsewhere, although the cross enclosed within a circle is common.

Links with Jerusalem

The stepped base of the high cross, the capstone and the idea of the jewelled cross all relate back to Jerusalem. Constantine, with his mother St Helena, in the fourth century had the Church of the Resurrection built over the Holy Sepulchre in Jerusalem. The stepped base refers to Golgotha close at hand, the place of the skull and the site of the Crucifixion *(fig. 24).* We know from the accounts of early pilgrims that a great cross was erected there with steps leading up to it.

Fig. 24

Russian tombstone, 1781, with carving of Golgotha

The tomb of Christ was enclosed in a small house 'adorned with choice columns and much ornament' (Eusebius, *Life of Constantine*). These were destroyed in the seventh century when the Persians invaded Palestine but we know about them through the accounts of pilgrims who flocked to visit the shrines from all over Christendom. Pilgrims to the Holy Land also brought back models and souvenirs, and particularly interesting are the early flasks stamped with pictures of the holy places *(fig. 25).* The story of the finding of the True Cross by St Helena further concentrated attention on Jerusalem.

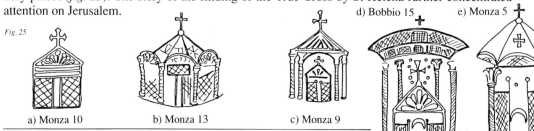

Fig. 25

a) Monza 10   b) Monza 13   c) Monza 9   d) Bobbio 15   e) Monza 5

Views of the Church of the Holy Sepulchre at Jerusalem on ampullae or pilgrim flasks from the Holy Land, sixth century, following Grabar.

An early sixth century account by a pilgrim describes the church built by Constantine. 'And going from there into Golgotha there is a great court where the Lord was crucified. There is a silver screen round this Mount, and a kind of flint has been left on the Mount. It has silver doors where the Cross of the Lord has been displayed, all adorned with gold and gems and the sky open above.'[6] The 'golden sky' of another reading is thought to indicate that there was a canopy or baldacchino, perhaps decorated with stars, above the cross. The cross adorned with gold and gems at Jerusalem may well be the inspiration for the stone imitation of metalwork, inlaid with gems, which is such an extraordinary feature of the Ahenny group of crosses. Well known representations of jewelled crosses occur elsewhere in mosaics. The jewelled cross at Jerusalem appears in the view of the Holy City in the apse of S Pudenziana in Rome of about 400, while in the sixth century mosaic in the apse of S Apollinare in Classe at Ravenna the bust of Christ, ringed by pearls, is at the centre of the splendid cross filling the starry sky.

It is Adamnan, ninth abbot of Iona (679–704), who has left us the best description of the buildings at Jerusalem in the seventh century in his work, *On the Holy Places (De Locis Sanctis)*. He got his information from Bishop Arculf who had lived in the city for nine months. By this time the Holy Land had recovered from the upheavals earlier in the century, and Arculf sketched plans of the sepulchre and the church built over it on a waxed tablet for Adamnan and the community at Iona around the year 683 *(plate VIII)*. Adamnan mentions the church 'on the site which in Hebrew is called Golgotha.

Plate VIII: Sketch of the Church of the Holy Sepulchre and its surroundings, from Adamnan's *De Locis Sanctis*. Vienna Cod. 458, fol. 4v

Bobbio 6

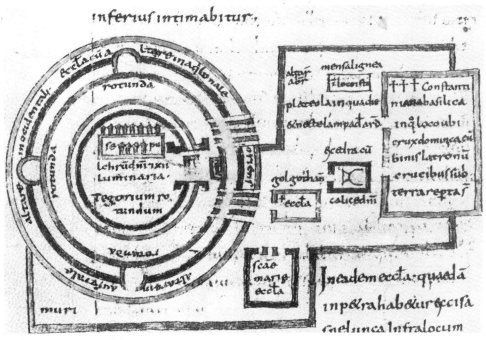

From the roof hangs a large bronze wheel for lamps, and below it stands a great silver cross, fixed in the same socket as the wooden cross on which the Saviour of mankind once suffered.'[7] Adamnan gives descriptions and plans which build up a remarkably detailed and clear picture of the holy places.

Just as the steps at the base of the high cross are linked to the steps up the hill of Golgotha, so the cap-stone or house-shape on the top of the cross is linked to the small shrine or house built by Constantine to mark the place of Christ's resurrection. Two types of cap-stone are found on the crosses. The majority are in the shape of a small house or church, with a shingled roof and finials, like the picture of Solomon's temple in the illustration of the temptation of Christ in the *Book of Kells* (fol. 202v) *(fig. 13)*. The other type occurs on the small group of crosses in the neighbourhood of Slievenamon and takes the form of a beehive shape. On analogy with the small church buildings on top of the scripture crosses which have been identified as simulating the Holy Sepulchre, the cap-stones of the Ahenny crosses must also represent buildings, possibly a canopy or a dome.[8] A dome was the actual shape of the building erected above the Holy Sepulchre.

A parallel exists in Georgia where the caps of medieval pre-altar crosses are of similar shape, like a canopy *(fig. 26 and plate IX)*. Huge pre-altar crosses of wood, covered with metal plates, still survive in churches in Svanetia. The symbolic sanctuary of the Holy Sepulchre proclaimed victory over death and the Triumph of the Cross. The caps of all the crosses accordingly stand for Sion, the Heavenly City and the New Jerusalem.

From all these considerations it appears that the Irish crosses are part of a Christian tradition which was widespread at one time. Ireland was left in relative isolation on the edge of Europe when neighbouring countries reverted to paganism in the fifth and sixth centuries following the barbarian invasions. The Church, unhindered in Ireland, went on from strength to strength, while scholarship flourished and art developed in an entirely original way. So it came about that the high crosses carved in the ninth and tenth centuries conserve much earlier features and are survivors of a stage largely unrepresented in western sculpture. The Irish crosses are important in the whole perspective of Christian art.

Plate IX: Cross-cap, Lagurka, Georgia, twelfth century

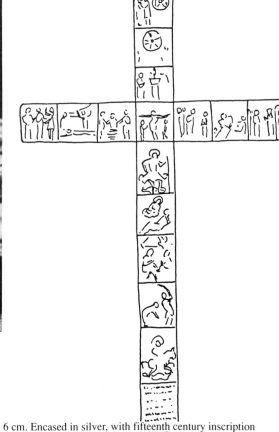

Fig. 26 Georgian pre-altar cross from Goridjvari, 168 x 85 x 6 cm. Encased in silver, with fifteenth century inscription and scenes from the life of St George; cap thirteenth century.

Past Studies On the Irish Crosses

The first major work on the Irish crosses was done by Henry O'Neill (1798–1880), an artist who was born in Clonmel but who spent most of his life in Dublin. His *Illustrations of the Most Interesting of the Sculptured Crosses of Ancient Ireland* came out in 1857, consisting of thirty-six coloured lithographs drawn to scale. Accompanying this work was *An Essay on Ancient Irish Art and Descriptions of the Prints*, given free of charge to avoid the compulsory presentation of copies to the Copyright Libraries, a practice which O'Neill considered to be a form of 'blackmail on literary industry'. After one hundred and fifty years, O'Neill's lithographs still command respect and admiration. There is a great deal to be learned from the appearance of the monuments as he shows them. Some of the crosses have been reassembled since his time. In any case until recently moss and lichen obscured the relief on carved surfaces so that it was sometimes impossible to make out the subjects of figured scenes. In spite of this O'Neill's work stands on its own merit.

Margaret Stokes (1832–1900) was the next to advance the study. She was the chief pioneer of early Irish art. In the nineteenth century a small group of scholars led by George Petrie, William Reeves and Lord Dunraven, had been investigating Irish antiquities. Margaret Stokes grew up in this background as these men were intimate friends of her father, a distinguished physician with antiquarian interests. She devoted the latter half of her life to the elucidation of the growth of Celtic art. Her best known work, written for the South Kensington set of handbooks, is *Early Christian Art in Ireland* (1886), which remained a standard text for many years. Later she embarked on a series illustrating *The High Crosses of Ireland* but only the first instalment was completed before her death. *High Crosses of Castledermot and Durrow* was published in 1898 under the auspices of the Royal Irish Academy. A second instalment, including her notes on Moone, Drumcliff, Termonfechin and Killamery, was published posthumously in 1901.

Following Margaret Stokes' work on the crosses, Henry S. Crawford compiled an admirable sequence of inventories and a handbook, *Carved Ornament from Irish Monuments* (1926). The latter is a valuable source of detailed information in spite of its slim dimensions. His reconstructions of panels to their former unweathered state are particularly useful.

The late 1920s saw the first publications on Irish crosses by Arthur Kingsley Porter (1883–1933), the distinguished American art historian and professor at Harvard.

From early on he had been interested in Romanesque sculpture. His *Romanesque Sculpture of the Pilgrimage Roads* came out in 1923 and the introduction to his *Spanish Romanesque Sculpture* (1928) draws attention to the importance of Irish carvings in the whole European setting. It was his search for early medieval sculpture which eventually brought him to live in Ireland. Unfortunately Kingsley Porter was cut down in his prime, and his stimulating book, *The Crosses and Culture of Ireland* (five lectures he delivered at the Metropolitan Museum of Art in New York in 1930), represents a provisional and unfinished stage in his work. In *Aesthetics and History in the Visual Arts* his friend, Bernard Berenson remarks that if Kingsley Porter 'had not been cut off in the midst of his efforts, he might have attempted to prove ... that monumental sculpture revived in Ireland and started the French on a course that led straight to Chartres and Rheims'.

It was Kingsley Porter's writings which provoked the first major article on the origins of Irish iconography by Françoise Henry (1902–1982). She was the French art historian and archaeologist whose life was devoted to the study of early Irish art. A student of Focillon in Paris, sculpture was of central importance to her work. Her doctoral thesis, *La Sculpture Irlandaise pendant les douze premiers siècles de l'ère chrétienne*, published in 1933, is a major survey of the great carved crosses and ecclesiastical sculpture of Ireland. She had already set out a basic chronological framework for the high crosses in the 1930 iconography paper. In all the following work this framework remained constant. It has been challenged over the years but has never been decisively breached. A recent proposal to reassess the date of the scripture crosses led to her final investigation: 'Around an Inscription: The Cross of the Scriptures at Clonmacnois', *(JRSAI* 1980). Here, with the help of the sculptor Domhnall Ó Murchadha, she was able effectively to confirm the traditionally accepted early tenth century date. Her *Irish High Crosses* (1964), published for the Cultural Relations Committee of Ireland, is a splendid basis for an introduction to the subject. She worked indefatigably, expanding the whole field and making many discoveries.

Helen M. Roe (1895–1988) excelled in regional studies of high crosses. Her short guides are invaluable for field trips. Her work for local societies went hand in hand with remarkable publications on iconography, for which she had a special affinity. Her achievements were honoured in 1987 in *Figures from the Past. Studies on figurative art in Christian Ireland*, a wide-ranging collection of papers edited by E. Rynne.

The publication of *Figures from the Past* reflects the enormous growth of interest in the high crosses. With local societies, surveys and conferences devoted entirely to sculpture, many different aspects are now being researched. Studies on the crosses in the last decade have expanded by leaps and bounds.

Notes

1 Kelly, D., 'Irish High Crosses: some evidence from the plainer examples', *JRSAI* 116, 1986, pp. 51–67.

2 Ó Ríordáin, S.P., 'The Genesis of the Celtic Cross', *Féilscríbhinn Torna*, ed. Pender, S., Cork 1947, pp. 108 –114.

3 Plummer, C., 'Metrical Litany of the Virgin Mary', *Irish Litanies*, London 1925, pp. 96–97.

4 Lionard, P., 'Early Irish Grave Slabs', *PRIA* 1961, C, 5, pp. 95 sq. Fig.16:11.

5 O'Dwyer, P., *Céli Dé, spiritual reform in Ireland 750–900*, Dublin 1981, p.156.

6 Wilkinson, J., *Jerusalem Pilgrims before the Crusades*, Warminster 1977, p.59.

7 *Ibid.*, p.97.

8 Richardson, H., 'The Concept of the High Cross', *Ireland and Europe, the Early Church*, ed. Ní Chatháin, P. and Richter, M., Stuttgart 1984, pp. 127–134.

Catalogue of Crosses and Illustrations

Entries are listed alphabetically with a map reference and short description. Measurements give only an approximation of height. The intention is to give a wide coverage of crosses to provide a basic source of illustrations for students. However the list of monuments is far from being all-inclusive.

Explanations of the figured scenes are often a matter of conjecture and several solutions may fit the case. Sometimes the meaning remains obscure. Generally accepted readings are given, or the suggestions of various authorities are referred to individually, using their initials. The scenes are normally read upwards, starting from the bottom.

There has been a great increase in publication and work on the crosses during the last years. To avoid confusion only one or two references are given in the catalogue.

A short bibliography can be found at the end. New information and discoveries are constantly changing the situation.

Abbreviations
HC – Henry S. Crawford; PH – Peter Harbison; FH – Françoise Henry; RASM – R.A.S. Macalister; KP – A. Kingsley Porter; HMR – Helen M. Roe; MS – Margaret Stokes.
JGAHS – Journal of the Galway Archaeological and Historical Society.
JRSAI – Journal of the Royal Society of Antiquaries of Ireland.
PRIA – Proceedings of the Royal Irish Academy.
UJA – Ulster Journal of Archaeology

Ahenny, Co. Tipperary *S 41 29 (Plates 1–6, 10-13)*
Monastic site of Kilclispeen or church of St Crispin, 4 miles north of Carrick-on- Suir. In the graveyard are two decorated crosses of sandstone and a cross-base. No historical information. F. Henry considers the Ahenny and neighbouring crosses to be the earliest of the ringed high crosses, dating to the eighth century through parallel designs in metalwork. Another view puts them a century later or more. They are characterised by overall metallic ornament with sparse figure subjects.

North Cross *(Plates 1–6)*
Height 3.65 m.   Four figured scenes on base only.

N side –   Procession with chariot. Translation of relics (HMR)

S   –   Funeral procession. Ecclesiastic with a ringed processional cross walks in front of a horse bearing a headless body. Ravens attack the corpse. At the rear a man carries the head which is seen in full face.
              Identified by KP and RASM as funeral of Cormac Mac Cuilennáin, Bishop-King of Munster, killed at the Battle of Bealach Mughna (Ballaghmoon), Co. Kildare in 908 Cf. the same incident on Dromiskin Cross.

E   –   Adam naming the animals (HC)

W   –   Mission of the Apostles (HMR); Seven Bishops (local tradition – MS)

South Cross *(Plates 10–13)*
Height: 3.35 m   All ornament, except for figured scenes on 4 sides of the base, badly worn. Base divided by a cross in relief.

N side –   Hunting scenes

E   –   includes Daniel in the Lions' Den on left

S   –   includes Fall of Man on left

Refs: Roe 1958; Edwards 1983

29

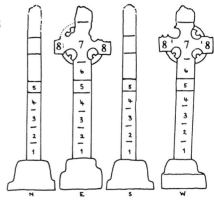

Arboe, Co. Tyrone *H 96 76 (Plates 14–22)*
Monastic site associated with St Colman. Tall sandstone cross, badly weathered, at entrance to graveyard beside Lough Neagh. Height: 5.6 m. approx. All sides carved in panels, mainly figured subjects. Tenth century.
Refs: Roe 1956; Hamlin 1982 *v.* under Whitelock

N 1 Baptism of Christ ?
   2 Unidentified
   3 Massacre of the Innocents
   4 Unidentified
   5 Decoration

E 1 Adam and Eve
   2 Sacrifice of Isaac
   3 Daniel in the Lions' Den
   4 Three children in fiery furnace
   5 Ornament
   6 Christ with the Apostles? (HMR)
   7 Last Judgement, with weighing of
     souls and fire of hell below
   8 Blessed and Damned? (HMR)

S 1 Cain and Abel
   2 David and the Lion
   3 David and Goliath
   4 The raven brings bread to St Paul and St Anthony
   5 Decoration

W 1 Adoration of the Magi
   2 Wedding at Cana
   3 Multiplication of loaves and fishes
   4 Entry into Jerusalem
   5 Ornament
   6 Arrest of Christ or *Ecce Homo*
   7 Crucifixion; angels support Christ's head
   8 Scenes of the Passion?

Armagh, Co. Armagh *H 87 45 (plates 7-9)*
In St Patrick's Cathedral (Church of Ireland) the Market Cross, large part of sandstone cross and fragment of its cross-head. Badly damaged. Probably tenth century.
Refs: Roe 1955

N 1 Three Children in fiery furnace
   2 Ornament
   3 Raven brings bread to St Paul and
      St Anthony
   4 Two standing figures

E 1 Adam and Eve
   2 Noah's Ark, with dove
   3 Sacrifice of Isaac
   4 Partially destroyed
   5 Three figures; perhaps Arrest of
      Christ or Moses, Aaron and Hur (KP)
Cross-head   Crucifixion
W   –   Christ in glory

S 1 Two persons; David and Jonathan?
      (HMR)
   2 David and Goliath
   3 David and the Lion
   4 Uncertain

W 1 Annunciation to the Shepherds
   2 Adoration of the Magi
   3 Baptism of Christ
   4 Obscure

East

Bealin, Co. Westmeath *N 10 43 (Plates 23–26)*
Decorated cross dated by an inscription to about 800, now on a small hill in Twyford Demesne, 3 miles
north-east of Athlone, but probably from Clonmacnois originally. Height: 2.05m. Inscription on lowest
panel of W face, carved in raised letters of almost 2mm., reads: Pray for Tuathgall who caused this
cross to be made. An abbot of Clonmacnois of this name died in 810 according to the *Annals of Ulster*.
N side   –   Hunting scene; a stag and wolfhound; horseman with spear.
E   –   A lion at the bottom, with scroll of interlocked creatures running up the shaft.
Refs: Hicks 1980
Bealin inscription after F. Henry

Boho, Co. Fermanagh *H 12 46 (Plate 27)*
In Toneel graveyard, shaft of a sandstone cross, and part of its head. Mainly ornament, but Adam and
Eve on one face and Baptism of Christ on the other. There are holes in the narrow sides, perhaps for
additions. Early photograph by H.S.Crawford.

Carndonagh, Co. Donegal   *C 46 45 (plates 28–33)*
St Patrick's Cross of red sandstone without a ring, accompanied by two small pillars (*plates 28–31*),
stands at the roadside beside the graveyard of the Church of Ireland church. Height: *circa* 2.50 m.
Broad ribbon interlace weaves the cross carved in shallow relief on both faces. The ribbon, edged on
either side by a narrow border, compares closely to interlace in the *Book of Durrow* (*circa* 650).
Following F. Henry a seventh century date for the cross seems most likely; cf. Stevenson tenth century,
and Harbison ninth century.
N face   –   Plain
S   –   single figures, perhaps Apostles
E   –   A group of three birds beneath the cross arms
               Below: Figure of Christ with four figures. Interpreted as the Crucifixion; or Christ in glory
               with right hand raised in blessing (FH). Note bird above head of lower right figure, (bad
               thief – PH).
W   –   Interlace

North Pillar – Height: 0.8m.
N   –   Bird and fish
S   –   Spirals
E   –   David the Warrior
W   –   David the Psalmist (with harp)

South Pillar – Height: 0.8 m.
N   Above, head in profile, fish; perhaps Jonah
S   Threefold knot; Horned (?) figure carrying a hammer
E   Human head
W   Ecclesiastic with bell, book and crosier

Carndonagh Cross-pillar *(Plates 32-33)*
1.68 m. high, in the graveyard where there is also a lintel carved with a ringed cross in relief.
N   –   Interlace
S   Key pattern
E   Crucifixion with two figures below, inscribed with crosses
W   Flabellum or liturgical fan, inset with marigold pattern, flanked by two ecclesiastics with
             crosiers
Refs: Stevenson 1956; Lacy 1983; Harbison 1986 *v.* under Higgitt

 N

Cashel, Co. Tipperary *S 07 41 (Plate 34)*
On the Rock of Cashel, south-west of ruined cathedral. St Patrick's Cross of local Drumbane sandstone
has stone supports on either side. Height: c. 2.28 m. Two full length figures in high relief on the broad
faces. Twelfth century. A replica now stands out-of-doors.
E   –   A bishop, probably St Patrick, standing on an animal's head
W   Crucifixion. Christ with outstretched arms and long robe.
Square base, very worn, has Urnes-style interlace on E side.

Castledermot, Co. Kildare *S 78 95 (Plates 35–42)*
Two granite crosses in the Church of Ireland graveyard at Dísert Diarmada founded in 812. Both
probably ninth century. Characterised by figured scenes in rather stiff panels and bold spiral ornament.
N Cross height: 3.12 m.
S Cross height 3.66 m.
Refs: Flower 1954; de Bhaldraithe; Herity 1987 *v.* under Rynne

Castledermot North Cross *(plates 35–38)*

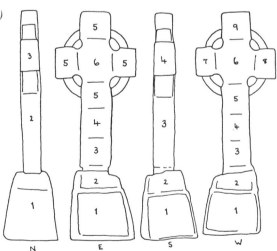

N	1	Bound crouching figure; evil?	S	1	Miracle of loaves and fishes
	2	Running spiral		2	Ornament
	3	One figure, at prayer (MS)		3	Broad interlace
				4	Key pattern

E	1	Spirals	W	1	Spirals
	2	Ornament		2	Ornament
	3	Two figures		3	Three figures; Emmaus? (KP)
	4	Raven brings bread to St. Paul and St. Anthony		4	Temptation of St Anthony?
	5	Apostles		5	Daniel in the Lions' Den
	6	Crucifixion		6	Fall of Man
				7	David the Psalmist
				8	Sacrifice of Isaac
				9	Fall of Simon Magus (KP)

Castledermot South Cross *(plates 39–42)*

N	1	Fighting figures	S	1	Miracles of loaves and fishes
	2	Figure in prayer		2	Figures of the Apostles in pairs
	3	Two figures (?)		3	Single figure
	4	Two figures, Massacre of Innocents (FH)		4	Spirals
	5	Warrior			
	6	Jacob and the Angel			
	7	Single figure			
	8	Spirals			

W	1	Hunting scene
	2	Daniel in Lions' Den
	3	Temptation of St Anthony, Susannah and the elders?
	4	Adam and Eve
	5	Raven brings bread to St Paul and St Anthony
	6a	Three figures, The Three Children?
	6	Crucifixion
	7	David the Psalmist
	8	Sacrifice of Isaac
	9	Three figures, Emmaus (KP)
	10	Moses, Aaron and Hur (KP)

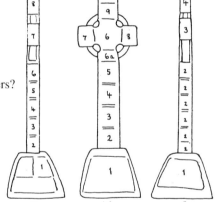

Castlekieran, Co. Meath *N 69 77 (Plate 43)*
Three sandstone termon or boundary crosses in the graveyard, with another base nearby.
N Cross height: 3.37m

Clogher, Co.Tyrone *H 54 51 (Plates 45–48)*
Two sandstone crosses found in the graveyard of St Macartan's Cathedral and re-erected. Probably ninth/tenth century. Also a sundial, probably seventh century, now moved indoors to the cathedral porch. N Cross height: 2.30 m.; S Cross height: 2.75 m.

The sundial has broad ribbon interlace below the dial and a fish at the bottom. The reverse side shows a 'face cross' with head of Christ and breast-plate of interlace. Height: 1.47 m.
Refs: Roe 1960; Hamlin 1987 *v.* under Rynne.

Clonca, Culdaff, Co. Donegal *C 52 47 (Plates 49–50)*
Shaft of cross and part of one arm, recently reattached, in the graveyard near the ruined church of St
Buodan. Height: 3.95 m.
E face   – at top, Miracle of Loaves and Fishes; (orans figure i.e. in prayer, on the arm not shown in
photograph)
W   – The hermits, St Paul and St Anthony with lions and crosiers
Refs: Lacy 1983; Harbison 1986 *v.* under Higgitt.

Clones, Co. Monaghan *H 50 26 (Plates 51–54)*
Early monastic foundation of St Tigernach. Market Cross on the Diamond, shaft of one sandstone cross
and head of another, mounted together. Tenth century. Height: 4.57 m. The narrow sides carry ornament
while the biblical scenes are linked to the Ulster group of crosses, Donaghmore, Arboe, Armagh, etc.

N			S		
	1	Adoration of Magi (FH)		1	Fall of Man
	2	Wedding at Cana		2	Sacrifice of Isaac
	3	Multiplication of loaves and fishes		3	Daniel in the Lions' Den
		(KP)		4	Entry into Jerusalem?
	4	Ornament		5	Daniel in the Lions' Den
	5	Crucifixion		5a	Arrest?
				5b	Pilate washing his hands? (KP)
E		Ornament	W		Angel at end of arm. Ornament

Clonmacnois, Co. Offaly *N 01 31 (Plates 44, 55–66)*
There was a sculpture workshop associated with the large important monastery on the Shannon founded
by St Ciaran in the sixth century. Most notable are the memorial slabs or recumbent grave-stones,
bearing crosses of many forms and often with inscriptions dating from the eighth to the twelfth
centuries. High crosses on the site are the Cross of the Scriptures, the N Cross and the S Cross, along
with a number of fragments. A shaft of a cross, once at Banagher, originally came from Clonmacnois.

North Cross *(Plates 55–57)*
Sandstone shaft of squarish section, 36 x 31 cm., with tenon for another portion. Height: roughly 2 m.
Carved on three sides with panels, mainly of ornament.
N face   – at top, human figure and interlacing, damaged; two lions below
S   – Lion in top panel; cross-legged figure in second panel from bottom
W   – Interlace

South Cross *(Plates 59–62)*
Sandstone cross with hatched moulding, *circa* 3.65 m. high, south-east of the Cathedral. Probably the
earliest cross now on the site, it marks a transition from the Ahenny group of ornamented crosses to the
crosses with biblical scenes, and has links with Iona in the adoption of raised bosses. Ninth century.
Base very worn.
S face   – Base: Fall of Man in left hand panel
E   – Base: Horsemen; shaft: panel of inhabited vinescroll (vine with birds and animals in the
             branches)
W   – Base: Procession of horsemen; shaft: Crucifixion; mutilated inscription on lowest panel.
Refs: Edwards 1986 *v.* Higgitt; Ó Murchadha 1988

West Cross *(Plate 58)*
Shaft, 92 cm. high, 18 cm. wide. Undecorated on reverse.
N face   – A lion biting its tail; a horseman; two lions

Banagher Cross *(Plate 44)*
Shaft of a cross, moved from Clonmacnois to Banagher, taken to the National Museum, Dublin.
1.52 m.high, 18 cm. wide.
Front   – Human interlace; deer caught in a trap; horseman (ecclesiastic) with crosier; lion
Back   3 panels: 1) interlace with two men, 2) lion, 3) interlace
Refs: Hicks 1980

Cross of the Scriptures or King Flann's Cross *(Plates 63–66)*
In front of the west door of the Cathedral. Made from one block of hard, buff coloured millstone grit,
3.90 m. high. Carved in panels on all four sides. Dated to about 901 by the inscription in two lines on
the E and W faces, naming Flann Sinna, King of Ireland 879 – 916.
Refs: Henry 1980; Ó Murchadha 1980
Many of the scenes are difficult to interpret. KP suggested that some of them illustrate the life of St
Patrick.

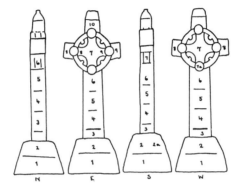

N   1   Animals
     2   Griffins and a centaur?
     3   St Michael fighting the devil (FH)
          Christ piercing Satan (MS)
     4   Figure playing the flute, with cats;
          David?
     5   St Matthew (FH)
     6   Heads within serpent interlace

E   1   Two chariots with horses
     2   Three horsemen; Magi? (KP)
     3   Inscription
     4   The foundation of Clonmacnois
          with St Ciaran and Dermot
     5   Two richly dressed, bearded men
     6   Mission to the Apostles (MS)
          Ecce Homo?
     7   Last Judgement, with angel blowing
          trumpet (left) and devil (right)
     8   Blessed
     9   Damned
     10   The Trinity; Moses, Aaron and Hur; Colmcille between two angels (KP)?

S   1   Hunting scene
     2   Four figures
     2a   Jacob and the Angel
     3   Two centaurs in medallions
     4   Human interlace
     5   Harpist with lion, David?
     6   St John (FH)
     7   Heads within serpent interlace

W   1   Uncertain subjects
     2   Uncertain subjects
     3   Inscription
     4   Soldiers guarding the tomb of Christ
     5   Arrest of Christ
     6   Flagellation, *Ecce Homo*?
     7   Crucifixion
     7a   Dove
     8   Uncertain

Donaghmore, Co. Down *J 10 35 (plates 67–68)*
Small granite cross re-erected in the graveyard of the Church of Ireland church. It is 3 m. high, carved on four sides with figures not enclosed in panels. Evenly stepped base. Ninth/tenth century. The cap and cross-head are from one block of stone, the shaft from another.

S face   –   David the Psalmist
E   Includes scenes from the life of David, David holding Goliath's head on a pole, David and the Lion.
W   Adam and Eve; four fish; the Ark; 2 groups of 2 figures. Head – Crucifixion with thief on either arm

Donaghmore, Co. Tyrone *H 77 65 (plates 71–76)*
Founded by St Patrick in tradition. Large sandstone cross, badly weathered, prominently sited at the road junction at the W end of the village, beside the graveyard wall. 4.80 m. high. Possibly parts of two crosses or central portion missing. Ninth/tenth century in date. Old Testament scenes on one face, New Testament on the other, with ornament on the sides.

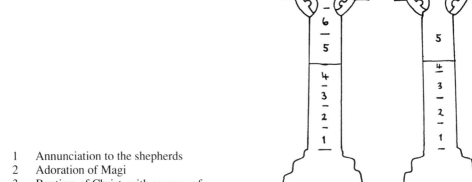

E   1   Annunciation to the shepherds
    2   Adoration of Magi
    3   Baptism of Christ, with sources of Jordan at left
    4   Wedding at Cana (HMR)
    5   Multiplication of loaves and fishes (HMR)
    6   Arrest of Christ or *Ecce Homo*
    7   Crucifixion, angels support Christ's head.
    8   Three figures?
Refs: Roe 1956

W   1   Fall of Man
    2   Cain and Abel, Christ on right (HMR)
    3   Sacrifice of Isaac
    4   Obscure
    5   Cross-Head: Ornament

Downpatrick, Co. Down *J 48 44 (plates 69–70)*
Site associated with St Patrick. Granite cross, badly weathered, outside the Cathedral but formerly in the town. Height: 3.35 m. Crucifixion on E side of head. Ninth/tenth century.

Dromiskin, Co.Louth *0 05 98 (plates 104–105)*
Cross-head of granite mounted on modern shaft in the graveyard. Bold mouldings enclose ornament on one face, while the other, shown half buried in the 1907 photograph, has a huntsman, hound and deer on the left arm, and on the right arm the same subject that is depicted on the base of the N Cross, Ahenny. A headless body is carried on a horse, preceded by a man bearing the head. Porter suggests it is the body of Cormac mac Cuilennáin killed in 908. Four dragon-like creatures unwind from the central boss.

Drumcliff, Co. Sligo *G 68 42 (plates 77–80)*
Cross of sandstone, 3.95 m. high, in the graveyard. Carved with a lively mixture of figure scenes and ornament, framed by a pellet moulding on the broad faces. Eleventh century?

N and S — A square mortice hole on each of the narrow sides. Ornament on shaft, with animals and frog-like creatures on ring. Figures on S end of arm interpreted as Virgin and Child by MS.

E   Fall of Man; Lion-like animal in high relief;
                Cain and Abel (MS) or sacrifice of Isaac;
                Daniel in the Lions' Den; Christ in glory or
                Last Judgement at centre of the head.

W   Interlace; Presentation in the Temple; large animal;
                3 figures – *Ecce Homo* or Arrest of Christ (?);
                2 figures – Mary and John (MS); Crucifixion

Duleek, Co. Meath *0 04 69 (plates 81–84)*
Early foundation in time of St Patrick. North Cross, small sandstone cross at entrance to the graveyard where there is also the head of another cross. Carved in panels on all four sides, figure subjects predominate on the W face. Height: 1.80 m., base buried; tenon for cap-stone.

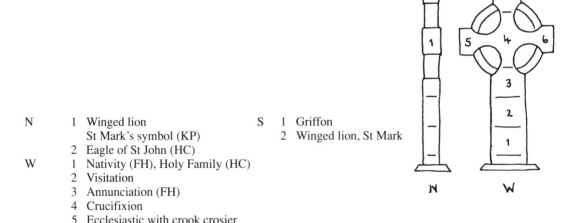

N   1   Winged lion
             St Mark's symbol (KP)
      2   Eagle of St John (HC)
W   1   Nativity (FH), Holy Family (HC)
      2   Visitation
      3   Annunciation (FH)
      4   Crucifixion
      5   Ecclesiastic with crook crosier
      6   Ecclesiastic with tau crosier
      7   Raven brings bread to St Paul and St Anthony

S   1   Griffon
       2   Winged lion, St Mark

Durrow, Co. Offaly *N 32 31 (plates 85–88, 127)*
At Durrow Abbey, three and a half miles north of Tullamore, on the site of an early Columban monastery. The West Cross, 3.60 m. high, stands by the gate into the graveyard. It is grouped with the Monasterboice crosses and the Cross of the Scriptures at Clonmacnois. Inscriptions on the N and W faces were mutilated but have recently been re-read. The name of Máelsechnaill, King of Ireland, is included on the N face.

Refs: Ó Murchadha 1988.

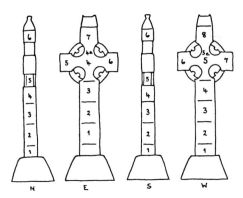

Durrow

N   1   Remains of inscription
     2   Jacob and the Angel
     3   8 spiral bosses
     4   Flight into Egypt
     5   Heads within serpent interlace
     6   Seated figure

E   1   Two seated figures with an open book,
          large central figure and two angels.
          Holy Trinity with angels (MS)?
     2   Interlace
     3   Sacrifice of Isaac
     4   Last Judgement, with angel blowing
          trumpet and angel in adoration
     4a   *Agnus Dei*
     5   David the Psalmist
     6   David and the lion
     7   Ornament

S   1   Winged lions or griffons
     2   Adam and Eve
     3   Cain and Abel
     4   Warrior with plaited beard and two dogs;
          David (HMR), Finn (KP)
     5   Heads within serpent interlace
     6   Horseman

W   1   Inscription
     2   Soldiers guarding the tomb of Christ
     3   Arrest of Christ
     4   *Ecce Homo*, or Arrest
     5   Crucifixion
     5a   Dove
     6   Denial of St Peter(KP)?
     7   Pilate washing his hands(KP)?
     8   Moses, Aaron and Hur?
          Judgement of Tara (KP)

Durrow Cross-head *(plate 127)*
The altered head of another cross, apparently once adapted as a gable finial on the church. It seems to mark a transition from the tenth century crosses towards the later twelfth century type.
Refs: Henry 1985

Dysert O'Dea, Co. Clare *R 28 85 (plates 89–92)*
To the east of the ruined church a ringless limestone cross of striking design, mid twelfth century. Height: 3.95 m. approx. There are small sockets at the ends of the cross arms. The interlace is of Urnes type.
N face   –   Base – The founding of a church
S   Base – Daniel in the Lions' Den
E   Crucifixion in high relief; figure of a bishop below, probably St Tola, founder of Dysert O'Dea
W   Base – Uncertain

Fahan, Co. Donegal *C 34 36 (plates 93–95)*
Four miles south of Buncrana. In the graveyard a splendid cross-slab, 2.1 m. high, associated with St Mura, early seventh century founder and patron. The slab is also considered to be seventh century with similar treatment to the Carndonagh Cross a little further north. The two broad faces are carved in low

relief with equal-armed crosses made of wide ribbons, the shaft extended like the handle of a flabellum or liturgical fan. The pedimental top contains 2 birds facing each other on the E face, while below the cross on the W face are two figures in profile bearing inscriptions in Irish on their garments, partially deciphered.

N   –   Inscription of *Gloria Patri* in Greek with formula 'glory and honour' accepted at the Council of Toledo in 633. Two short projections for some practical function are on the narrow sides at the level of the cross-arms.

S   Plain

Refs: Lacey 1983; Harbison 1986 *v.* under Higgitt

Gallen Priory, Co. Offaly *N 12 23 (plates 96–98)*
Near Ferbane. Several ornate cross-slabs and a group of recumbent grave-slabs.
Refs: Lionard 1961

Galloon, Co. Fermanagh *H 39 23 (plates 99–101)*
Remains of two crosses, E and W, in the graveyard on Galloon Island in Upper Lough Erne. Shafts both badly defaced, carved on all four sides, had inscriptions once. Fragments of two cross-heads, one in the care of the Department of the Environment. Subjects include:

East Cross *(plate 101)*
E face   –   Sacrifice of Isaac; interlace; 3 figures, perhaps Moses, Aaron and Hur; interlace
W   Adoration of the Magi; Baptism of Christ; St Paul and St Anthony receiving bread from the raven
Head   Daniel in the Lions' Den, with Crucifixion on reverse

West Cross *(plates 99–100)*
E face: uncertain; Daniel in the Lions' Den; Adam and Eve
Refs: Lowry-Corry 1934; Hamlin 1980

Glendalough, Co. Wicklow *T 13 97 (plates 102–103)*
Great monastery founded by St Kevin, with many early grave stones and carvings. The Market Cross, granite cross about 2 m. high, once outside but now in the Visitors' Centre in the care of the Office of Public Works. No ring, but billets at the angles of the arms. Figures in high relief on one face: 2 figures on the base; a bishop; Crucifixion. Twelfth century.

Graiguenamanagh, Co. Kilkenny *S 71 44 (plates 106–108)*
Two crosses from the neighbourhood of Ullard now in the graveyard of Duiske Abbey.
North Cross, from Ballyogan *(plates 107–108)*
Granite cross with solid ring, 2.30 m. high, with a high base.
E face   –   David the Psalmist; Sacrifice of Isaac: Fall of Man; Crucifixion
W   Ornament, with bottom panel Massacre of Innocents (FH), 2 figures at the top
South Cross, from Aghailten *(plate 106)*
Granite cross with solid ring, nearly 2 m. high, with the Crucifixion and panels of interlace.

Inishkeel, Co. Donegal *D 71 00 (plate 109)*
Near Naran, early monastic site with cross slabs and shaft of cross covered with broad interlace.

Kells, Co. Meath *N 74 76 (plates 111–124)*
Three crosses and a base (N Cross) in the Church of Ireland graveyard surrounding the church.
1) South Cross, called also the Cross of Kells, Cross of the Tower, or **Cross of Patrick and Columba** *(plates 110–113)* seems to be the earliest, dating perhaps to the first decade of the ninth century when

the monks fled from Iona to Kells. A sandstone cross, 3.30 m. high, it stands beside the round tower. It is a monolith set on a base. The cap-stone is missing but there is a tenon for it. The cross is covered with a mixture of ornament and figure carving. It is the only cross to have the four symbols of the Evangelists surrounding Christ in glory. Inscription on upper part of the E face of the base reads:

PATRICII ET COLUMBE CR(UX)

N 1   Inhabited vine-scroll
   2   Samson and the lion (HC)
       David and the bear (HMR)
   3   St Peter and St Paul? (HMR)

E 1   Hunting scene or Noah bringing animals
       into the Ark
   2a Inscription
   2   Interlace
   3   Adam and Eve
   4   Cain and Abel
   5   Three Children with angel above and
       men stoking the furnace at each side
   6   Daniel in the Lions' Den
   7   Seven bosses, possibly loaves in Miracle
       scene, symbol of the Eucharist
   8   Sacrifice of Isaac
   9   Raven brings bread to St Paul and St Anthony. Griffon? at left
   10 Multiplication of loaves and fishes. Two fish in a cross shape, crowd or Apostles above, with
       David the Harpist seated at left and Christ on right.

S 1   Interlace
   2   Bird and animal motifs
   3   David and the lion
   4   Two animals; Lion attacking a lamb (HC)

W 1   Procession of horsemen and a chariot
   2   Interlacing men
   3   Crucifixion
   4   Apocalyptic Vision. Christ in glory with
       symbols of the four Evangelists
       a) Angel of St Matthew
       b) Lion of St Mark
       c) Calf of St Luke
       d) Eagle of St John
   5   *Agnus Dei* in a wreath
   6   Bosses

2) West Cross or Broken Cross (plates 115–118). Remnant of a tall sandstone cross, 3.50 m. high, covered with figured panels on the broad faces and panels of ornament on the narrow sides. Cf. St Matthew's Cross, Iona.

E 1   Baptism of Christ, with sources of
       River Jordan as discs
   2   Wedding at Cana
   3   David? Unidentified
   4   Uncertain; Presentation in the Temple?
       (HMR)
   5   Uncertain
   6   Entry into Jerusalem

W 1   Adam and Eve
   2   Noah's Ark
   3   Uncertain; Three Children? (HC)
   4   Brazen serpent? (FH)

3) East or Unfinished Cross *(plates 123–124).*
A sandstone cross blocked out and partially carved. Height: approx. 4.25 m.

Market Cross *(plates 119–122)*
In the centre of the town, a sandstone cross, height: 3.35m., badly damaged, carved with figured panels on all four sides.
Refs: Roe 1959

N 1 Birds, animals and centaurs
   2 Jacob and the Angel
   3 Uncertain
   4 Arrest of Christ (KP)?
   5 Central horned figure flanked by rampant animals
   6 Raven brings bread to St Paul and St Anthony; chalice at bottom centre.

E 1 Four horsemen with swords and shields
   2 Spirals
   3 Soldiers guarding the tomb of Christ
   4 Goliath; or Christ, Lord of Hosts (HMR)
   5 Adam and Eve
   6 Cain and Abel
   7 David the Psalmist or Anointing of David by Samuel (HMR)
   8 Daniel in the Lions' Den
   9 Sacrifice of Isaac
  10 Temptation of St Anthony (KP)? or Avarice (HMR)?
  11 Virgin and Child seated with standing figure

S 1 Battle scene
   2 Stag hunt?
   3 Massacre of Innocents (KP)
   4 Healing the blindman (HMR)
      God appears to Moses in the burning bush (FH)
   5 Moses receiving the law, with Hand of God at right
   6 David and the lion

W 1 Deer-hunt, or Noah with the animals
   2 Inscription of 1688 in English
   3 Adoration of the Magi
   4 Wedding at Cana
   5 Multiplication of loaves and fishes: bread on left and fish on right
   6 Crucifixion
   7 Unidentified, two ecclesiastics
   8 Fall of Simon Magus

Kilbroney, Co. Down *J 19 19 (plates 125–126)*
Granite cross in the graveyard, about 2.50 m. high, without a ring but with hollows carved at the angles of the cross on the W face. The entire W face covered with fret patterns.

   Nearby in the graveyard a small granite 'face-cross', 1 m. high *(plate 125)*. Probably an early carving re-used.

Kilfenora, Co. Clare *R 18 94 (plates 132–136)*
The Doorty Cross is near the ruined cathedral, in the graveyard where there are other smaller crosses, *v.* the *North Cross*, 2 m. high, which has interlace on the W of the cross-head. In a field just to the W is a splendid ringed cross, also of limestone and also of twelfth century date, 4.5 m. high approx.

Doorty Cross *(plates 132–134)*
E face   – Figure of a bishop in high relief, with winged creatures on either side. Christ as Abbot of the World (?) 2 ecclesiastics thrusting their crosiers, a crooked and a tau, into the beast below
W   Crucifixion on the head with birds at the angles.   Below – Entry into Jerusalem (?)

Cross in field *(plates 135–136)*
E face   – Crucifixion with lamb or lion above Christ's head
W   Ornamental designs
Refs: de Paor 1956

Kilkieran, Co. Kilkenny *S 42 27 (plates 137–145)*
3 miles north of Carrick-on-Suir. Three sandstone crosses in the graveyard and fragments of other carvings.

N or **Tall Cross** *(plates 138–139)*
Unique in shape, slender with very short arms. Height: 3.50 m. The base is circular. There are hatched mouldings and hollows above and below the cross-arms on the W face. There are shallow grooves on the wide faces of the shaft. A tenon remains on top.

E or **Plain Cross** *(plate 137)*
About 2.80 m. high, of the Ahenny type with mouldings and central boss but otherwise plain.

W or **Decorated Cross** *(plates 140–143)*
Cross of Ahenny type, 3.80 m. high, covered with ornament. A rare instance of imperfect interlace.
N face   – Base – includes 2 six-pointed stars
E   Base – 8 horsemen
W   Shaft, panel with 4 long necked beasts with small equal-armed cross in centre

Kilkieran fragments *(plates 144–145)*
2 pieces of carved stone: parts of a cross or possibly a stone shrine. Another part survives.

Refs: Roe 1958; Edwards 1983

Killamery, Co. Kilkenny *S 38 36 (plates 146–149)*
Sandstone cross with base in pronounced steps and gabled cap-stone, in the graveyard where there are also several inscribed recumbent grave-slabs. Height: 3.65 m. There are double mouldings on the narrow sides. Angular patterns predominate in the ornament but there are figured scenes also:
N arm end – 4 scenes, top left – Jacob and the Angel, top right – David and the Lion (HMR) Lower scenes uncertain
W face   – Crucifixion below the whirling disc; David and Samuel above (HMR); figured subject to left, huntsman with 3 dogs pursuing a stag; to right, a chariot procession, (translation of relics [HMR]) Worn inscription in relief on base of shaft has been read as:
             O͞R DO MÁELSECHNAILL A prayer for Máelsechnaill
Refs: Roe 1958

Killary, Co. Meath *N 88 83 (plates 150–152)*
West cross, in graveyard. Part of shaft in a circular base, height: 1.80 m. Cf. Broken Cross at Kells

N 1 Uncertain, Virgin and Child (HC)   S   Ornament in panels
   2 Interlace
   3 David the warrior (HMR)

E 1 Adam and Eve   W 1 Annunciation to the shepherds (FH)
   2 Noah's Ark   2 Baptism of Christ
   3 Sacrifice of Isaac   3 Adoration of Magi
   4 Daniel in the Lions' Den

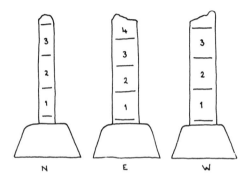

Kilnaboy, Co. Clare *R 27 91 (plate 110)*
Formerly near the road about one and a half miles north-west of Kilnaboy church. A tau cross of limestone, ending in two human heads. Shaft 43 cm. high, transom 69 cm. long.
Refs: Rynne 1967

Kilree, Co. Kilkenny *S 50 41 (plates 153–154)*
Sandstone cross, 2.75 m. high, a short distance from the round tower and ruined church. There is a tenon but no cap-stone. The surfaces, badly weathered, are covered with bosses and ornament. The narrow sides have double mouldings. Areas of small figured scenes:
S   – End of arm: 4 panels, top 2 uncertain; bottom left – Jacob and the Angel; bottom right – David and the Lion (HMR)
E   cross arms: Hunting scene and procession of horses
W   below central boss: Daniel in the Lions' Den
Refs: Roe 1958

Kinnitty Co. Offaly *N 20 06 (plates 129–131)*
Sandstone cross now in the grounds of Castle Bernard. Height: 2.40 m. with damaged cross-head. The capstone can be seen in H. Crawford's photographs. The broad faces, now N and S, but originally E and W probably, have inscriptions at the bottom which refer to King Máelsechnaill, 846–862.
N face – OR DO COLMAN DORRO ... IN CROSSA AR RIG HERENN
           OR DO RIG HERENN
           A prayer for Colman who made the cross for the King of Ireland. A prayer for the King of Ireland.
S   – OR DO RIG MAELSECHNAILL M̄ MAELRUANAID
           OROIT AR RIG HERENN
           A prayer for King Máelsechnaill son of Máelruanaid.
           A prayer for the king of Ireland.

Carvings are mainly interlace and ornament:

N   face/head –   7 bosses; 2 affronted birds; Adam and Eve
S   face/head –   Crucifixion with lance bearer and spongebearer; middle panel – interpreted by MS as
                   St Brendan of Clonfert giving a crosier to St Finan the Crooked, founder of Kinnitty
                   church

Refs: de Paor 1987 *v.* under Rynne; Ó Murchadha 1988

Lisnaskea, Co. Fermanagh *H 36 34*
Fragment of sandstone cross remounted in the market place.
E face   –   Adam and Eve
W   –   32 bosses

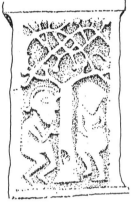

Lorrha, Co. Tipperary *M 92 05 (plate 128)*
Foundation of St Ruadhan, d.584. In the graveyard of the Church of Ireland the remains of two large
bases of the Ahenny type with stumps of shafts. Ornamented.
Cross-base, 1.60 m., has a procession of horses.

Mona Incha (Loch Cré), Co. Tipperary *S 17 88 (plate 155)*
Parts of two different crosses mounted together.
1) Base, ninth century, with carved horsemen
2) Upper part, Crucifixion in high relief; twelfth century

Monasterboice, Co. Louth *0 04 82 (plates 156–163)*
Early monastic site of St Buithe with three sandstone crosses and other carvings.

North Cross *(plate 163)*
Top portion of a ringed cross.
E face   –   Roundel with 16 spirals
W   Crucifixion

South cross *or* Cross of Muiredach *(plates 156–159)*
Named after an abbot, probably Muiredach mac Domhnaill, d.923. Majestic cross of fine micaceous
sandstone, 5.5 m. high, carved with figure subjects in strong relief on the broad faces and ornament on
the narrow sides of the shaft. The cap-stone is a separate stone, carved as a small church with finials at
either end of the roof. Inscription added at bottom of W face to the surface behind two cats carved in
high relief:
    OR DO MUIREDACH LASNDERNAD IN CHROS
A prayer for Muiredach under whose auspices the cross was made
Refs: Macalister 1946; Roe 1981

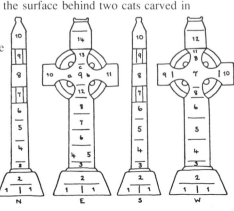

N 1 Ornament
2 Animals and centaurs
3 Two beard-pulling men
4-6 Interlace
7 Heads within serpents interlacing,
with Hand of God
8 Mocking of Christ or Flagellation
9 Interlace
10 The raven brings bread to St Paul and
St Anthony

S 1 Ornament, weathered
2 Horsemen and a chariot
3 Two animals, like cats
4 Interlacing men
5 Linked spirals
6 Inhabited vine-scroll
7 Heads within serpents interlacing. Two lions
8 Pilate washing his hands
9 Interlace
10 Entry into Jerusalem

E 1 Ornament
2 Signs of Zodiac (RASM)
3 Two animals
4 Adam and Eve
5 Cain and Abel
6 Scenes from life of David
7 Moses striking the rock
8 Adoration of the Magi with St Joseph
and star above Child
9-13 Last Judgement
9 Christ in Majesty
a) David the Psalmist with his harp on
which sits a dove (Holy Spirit)
b) Erythrian Sibyl (FH), Gabriel (HMR)
c) Dove (Holy Spirit) (RASM),
Phoenix (Resurrection) (HC)
10 The Blessed
11 The Damned, pushed by devils
12 St Michael weighing souls, a soul in the scales and a devil pulling on them below
13 Christ supported by angels (HMR), Three angels with the Book of Life(HC), or soul carried to
Heaven
14 Unidentified

W 1 Ornament
2 Signs of Zodiac? (RASM)
3 Cats and inscription
4 *Ecce Homo* or Arrest of Christ
5 Incredulity of St Thomas
6 Mission to the Apostles
7 Crucifixion, Longinus and Stephaton, sun
and moon, two angels support Christ's head
8 Bosses and snakes
9 Six figures
10 Soldiers at the tomb, Resurrection of
Christ
11 Two interlocked birds
12 Moses, Aaron and Hur

West Cross or Tall Cross *(plates 160–162)*
Near the round tower; almost 7 m. high. The cap-stone is very worn, as also the lower shaft. A band at
the top of the shaft marks the junction with the cross-head, carved from a separate block of stone. There
are figured scenes on the two broad faces, and figured panels mixed with panels of ornament on the
narrow sides. Tenth century.
Refs: as above.

N 1 Worn
2 Ornament
3 David the Warrior(HMR)
4 Bosses
5 Temptation of St Anthony?
Daniel in the Lions' Den?
6 Ornament
7 Winged animal
8 Key pattern

S 1 Ornament
2 Defaced
3 Linked spirals
4 Flight into Egypt
Presentation in Temple (RASM)
5 Animal interlace
6 Two figures holding a large rectangular object
7 Ornament
8 Winged animal
9 Key pattern

E		W	
1	Worn ornament	1	Worn decoration
2	David and the lion	2	Soldiers guarding the tomb
3	Sacrifice of Isaac	3	Baptism of Christ (RASM) Holy Women at the tomb (FH)
4	Worship of Golden Calf		
5	David with head of Goliath and David anointed by Samuel	4 – 7	Twelve Apostles?
		4	Emmaus (KP)
6	Goliath defying the armies of Israel	5	Mission of the Apostles?
7	Scene with a chariot – Elijah?	6	Incredulity of St Thomas (HMR)
8	Three children in fiery furnace	7	Arrest of Christ or *Ecce Homo* (HMR)
9	Christ, Lord of Hosts (HMR) The Second Coming a) – d) decorative bosses	8	Two soldiers, part of the Crucifixion scene; small bird in centre?
		9	Crucifixion; a) man with lamb b) man shearing sheep. (Atonement)
10	Temptation of St Anthony?(KP) Avarice (HMR)?	10	Mocking of Christ
11	Fall of Simon Magus	11	Kiss of Judas, Arrest
12	Walking on the Water	12	Uncertain, St Peter returning sword to scabbard?
13	Unidentified	13	Unidentified

Moone, Co. Kildare *S 79 93(plates 164–167)*

Moen Cholum Cille, site of an early Columban monastery. Unique, tall, slender cross of granite, 5.33 m. high, re-erected in the last century. Tenon for cap-stone at the top. Shaft squarish in section with separate middle portion. Base carved in shape of two truncated pyramids, covered on all four sides with figured scenes which follow a logical order, starting from the Fall of Man on the E face and continuing in a clockwise direction. Eighth/ninth century.
Refs: de Bhaldraithe; Stokes 1901

Also in the graveyard fragments of a second cross.

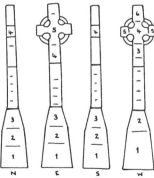

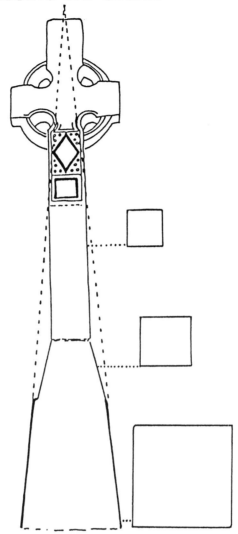

Sketch to show proportions of Cross of Moone, implying use of mathematics for Christian symbolism.

N   1   Monsters in the desert
     2   Temptation of St Anthony
     3   Raven brings bread for St Paul and
        St Anthony
        Shaft on all sides:
        Animals from the bestiary
     4   Figure

E   1   Daniel in the Lions' Den
     2   Sacrifice of Isaac
     3   Adam and Eve
     4   Heads and monsters intertwined
     5   Christ; with creature above, Dolphin (MS)

S   1   Multiplication of loaves and fishes
     2   Flight into Egypt
     3   Three children in the fiery furnace
     4   Figure

W   1   Twelve Apostles
     2   Crucifixion
     3   Lozenge, symbol of the Logos
        probably, filled with 4 spirals
     4   Whirligig
     5   Angels
     6   Spirals

Old Kilcullen, Co. Kildare *N 83 07 (plates 168–171)*
Early monastic site with round tower, portion of a granite cross and other cross fragments. The shaft, almost 2 m. high, is of squarish section and is carved in panels on all four sides. Ninth/tenth century.
Refs: Byrne 1987 *v.* under Rynne

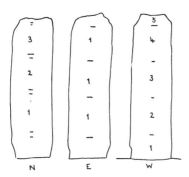

N   1   David and the lion
    2   Interlace
    3   Episode showing Mac Táil, 'son of adze', founder of Kilcullen, with crosier, bell and book, smiting the enemy

E   1   Twelve Apostles in 3 groups

S   Three panels of ornament, top – human interlace

W   1   Five heads
    2   Figures with ass, Flight into Egypt?
    3   Samson?
    4   Horseman blowing trumpet
    5   Lower part of Crucifixion?

Onaght, Temple Brecan, Inishmore, Aran, Co. Galway *L 81 12 (Plates 172–173)*
Shaft of cross with Crucifixion and interlacing. Other cross fragments. Old view taken by F. Henry
Refs: Waddell 1972 and 1981

Roscrea, Co. Tipperary *S 14 89 (plates 174–175)*
Cross, restored in part, in the graveyard beside St Cronan's church, near the main road. There are large figures in high relief on both faces. Animal interlace on shaft. At the bottom of the N and S sides is a large figure. Twelfth century.
E face   – An ecclesiastic, St Cronan
W   – Crucifixion

St Mullins, Co. Carlow *S 73 38 (plates 176–177)*
Early monastery of St Moling. South-east of the ruined church a granite cross with solid ring and cylindrical base. Portion of the shaft is missing, *v.* M. Stokes' reconstruction of the cross when complete.
Height: 2.10 m.
E face   – Crucifixion
W   – Ornament

Seir Kieran, Co. Offaly *N 14 02 (plates 178–179)*
Early foundation of St Ciaran of Saighir. In the Church of Ireland graveyard a large worn base, carved on four sides.
N face   – figure scenes include the Fall of Man, right below; the Three Children, middle below; Sacrifice of Isaac above it
Refs: Gilling 1937

Templeneiry, Co. Tipperary *R 95 29 (plates 196–197)*
St Berrihert's Kyle at Ardane. Part of a cross-head of red sandstone among a collection of slabs and carvings. Six pointed star within a circle at centre of the cross; Jacob and the Angel on left arm; other subjects uncertain. View of sanctuary by H.S. Crawford from the beginning of the century.
Refs: Ó hÉailidhe 1967 *v.* under Rynne

Termonfeckin, Co. Louth *0 14 80 (plates 180–183)*
Small sandstone cross, height: 2.60 m., in the Church of Ireland graveyard. Mainly ornament. Ninth/tenth century.
E face   – Crucifixion with lancebearer and spongebearer
W   – Christ in glory or Last Judgement

Tibberaghny, Co. Kilkenny *S 44 21 (plates 184–187)*
Near Piltown. In the south-east corner of the graveyard a stone pillar, carved on four sides, possibly part of a cross shaft. Height: 1.15 m.
N face   – Stag and lion
S   – 2 creatures or animals from the medieval bestiary, Manticora (HC) below, Hyaena (HMR) above
E   – Circular device including 7 spirals ending in 3 bird-like heads at the centre
W   – Centaur holding axes; 2 animals, lion and bull (?)
Refs: Roe 1958

Tihilly, Co. Offaly *(plates 188–191)*
Tech Theille, early monastic site one and a half miles south-west of Durrow. Damaged cross of fine-grained sandstone on a base of coarse conglomerate. Height: with capstone approx. 1.90 m. The narrow sides have panels of ornament.
E face   – Circle for 7 bosses; lowest panel of shaft – 2 birds interlocked, with human head below (HC)
W   – Crucifixion ; midway on shaft – Fall of Man
Refs: de Paor 1987 *v.* under Rynne

Tuam, Co. Galway *M 44 52 (plates 192–195)*
Twelfth century Market Cross in the centre of the town. Upper part with figures in high relief mounted on a larger shaft, possibly from another cross. There are mortice holes for additional pieces, perhaps for figures. Zoomorphic interlace of Urnes type. Figures at ends of the arms and on the base. Inscription on E side of base asks prayers for King Turlough O'Connor, 1106–1156; inscription on W side of base asks prayers for Aed O'Oissin, abbot and later archbishop of Tuam.
E face   – 5 standing figures
W   – Crucifixion

Ullard, Co. Kilkenny *S 72 48 (plates 198–199)*
Early site founded by St Fiacra. In the graveyard a granite cross (restored) with solid ring. Grouped with the Barrow Valley crosses.
E face   – base – ornament; figures of Apostles; Adam and Eve; cross-head – David the Psalmist; Crucifixion; Sacrifice of Isaac; 2 figures above, perhaps St Paul and St Anthony or Massacre of the Innocents (FH)

LIST OF PLATES

Plate I: St Martin's Cross, Iona (a and b)
Plate II: Crucifixion slab, Duvillaun
Plate III: Clonmacnois grave-slab, OR DO DAINÉIL
Plate IV: Stele from Haridj, sixth century
Plate V: Brdadzor, tall stele, sixth century
Plate VI: Odzun, south pillar from east, sixth century
Plate VII: Khatchkar, 1184, at Sanahin
Plate VIII: Sketch of the Church of the Holy Sepulchre and its surroundings, from Adamnan's *De Locis Sanctis*. Vienna Cod. 458, fol. 4v
Plate IX: Cross-cap, Lagurka, Georgia, twelfth century
Plate 1:   North Cross, Ahenny, east face
Plate 2:   North Cross, Ahenny, south face
Plate 3:   North Cross, Ahenny, west face
Plate 4:   North Cross, Ahenny, south base
Plate 5:   North Cross, Ahenny north shaft
Plate 6:   North Cross, Ahenny north base
Plate 7:   The 'Market' Cross, Armagh, east face
Plate 8:   The 'Market' Cross, Armagh, cross-head
Plate 9:   The 'Market' Cross, Armagh, detail of north face (St Paul and St Anthony)
Plate 10:   South Cross, Ahenny, north face
Plate 11:   South Cross, Ahenny, west face
Plate 12:   South Cross, Ahenny, south face
Plate 13:   South Cross, Ahenny, east face
Plate 14:   Arboe Cross, west face
Plate 15:   Arboe, south shaft
Plate 16:   Arboe, east face of crosshead
Plate 17:   Arboe, detail of east face (Adam and Eve)
Plate 18:   Arboe, detail of east face (Sacrifice of Isaac)
Plate 19:   Arboe, detail of east face (Daniel in the Lions' Den)
Plate 20:   Arboe, detail of east face (The Three Children in the Fiery Furnace)
Plate 21:   Arboe, detail of south face
Plate 22:   Arboe, detail of north face
Plate 23:   Bealin Cross, north face
Plate 24:   Bealin Cross, west face
Plate 25:   Bealin Cross, south face
Plate 26:   Bealin Cross, east face
Plate 27:   Boho Cross, detail of shaft showing the Fall of Man
Plate 28:   Carndonagh, Cross, and pillars, east face
Plate 29:   Carndonagh, north pillar from west
Plate 30:   Carndonagh, south pillar from west
Plate 31:   Carndonagh Cross, from south-west
Plate 32:   Carndonagh Cross-pillar, east face
Plate 33:   Carndonagh Cross-pillar, west face
Plate 34:   St Patrick's Cross, Cashel, east face
Plate 35:   Castledermot North Cross, base, north side
Plate 36:   Castledermot North Cross, east face
Plate 37:   Castledermot North Cross, south face
Plate 38:   Casltedermot North Cross, west face
Plate 39:   Castledermot South Cross, north face
Plate 40:   Castledermot South Cross, west face
Plate 41:   Castledermot South Cross, south face
Plate 42:   Castledermot South Cross, east face
Plate 43:   Castlekieran North Cross
Plate 44:   Shaft of cross, Banagher Cross, *v.* Clonmacnois
Plate 45:   South Cross, Clogher, from east
Plate 46:   North Cross, Clogher, from east
Plate 47:   Clogher Sun-dial, west face
Plate 48:   Clogher Sun-dial, east face
Plate 49:   Clonca Cross, west face
Plate 50:   Clonca Cross, east face
Plate 51:   Clones Cross, north face
Plate 52:   Clones Cross, east face
Plate 53:   Clones Cross, south face
Plate 54:   Clones Cross, west face

Plate 55:   Clonmacnois North Cross, north face
Plate 56:   Clonmacnois North Cross, west face
Plate 57:   Clonmacnois North Cross, south face
Plate 58:   Clonmacnois West Cross
Plate 59:   Clonmacnois South Cross, north face
Plate 60:   Clonmacnois South Cross, west face
Plate 61:   Clonmacnois South Cross, south face
Plate 62:   Clonmacnois South Cross, east face
Plate 63:   Clonmacnois, Cross of the Scriptures, north face
Plate 64:   Clonmacnois, Cross of the Scriptures, west face
Plate 65:   Clonmacnois, Cross of the Scriptures, south face
Plate 66:   Clonmacnois, Cross of the Scriptures, east face
Plate 67:   Donaghmore Cross (Co. Down), west face
Plate 68:   Donaghmore Cross (Co. Down), detail of west face
Plate 69:   Downpatrick Cross, west face
Plate 70:   Downpatrick Cross, east face
Plate 71:   Donaghmore Cross (Co. Tyrone), east face
Plate 72:   Donaghmore Cross (Co. Tyrone), west face, cross head
Plate 73:   Donaghmore Cross (Co. Tyrone), detail of west face, (Fall of Man)
Plate 74:   Donaghmore Cross (Co. Tyrone), detail of west face, (Cain and Abel)
Plate 75:   Donaghmore Cross (Co. Tyrone), detail of west face, (Sacrifice of Isaac)
Plate 76:   Donaghmore Cross (Co. Tyrone), south face, lower half
Plate 77:   Drumcliff Cross, north face
Plate 78:   Drumcliff Cross, west face
Plate 79:   Drumcliff Cross, south face
Plate 80:   Drumcliff Cross, east face
Plate 81:   Duleek Cross, north face
Plate 82:   Duleek Cross, west face
Plate 83:   Duleek Cross, south face
Plate 84:   Duleek Cross, east face
Plate 85:   Durrow Cross, north face
Plate 86:   Durrow Cross, west face
Plate 87:   Durrow Cross, south face
Plate 88:   Durrow Cross, east face
Plate 89:   Dysert O'Dea Cross, north face
Plate 90:   Dysert O'Dea Cross, west face
Plate 91:   Dysert O'Dea Cross, south face
Plate 92:   Dysert O'Dea Cross, east face
Plate 93:   Fahan Mura, Cross-slab, west face
Plate 94:   Fahan Mura, Cross-slab, east face
Plate 95:   Fahan Mura, Greek inscription
Plate 96:   Gallen Priory, detail of cross-slab
Plate 97:   Gallen Priory, cross-slab
Plate 98:   Gallen Priory, grave-slab with ringed cross
Plate 99:   Galloon West Cross, east face
Plate 100:   Galloon West Cross, head
Plate 101:   Galloon East Cross, west face
Plate 102:   Glendalough 'Market' Cross, west face
Plate 103:   Glendalough 'Market' Cross, east face
Plate 104:   Dromiskin Cross-head, east face
Plate 105:   Dromiskin Cross-head, west face
Plate 106:   Graiguenamanagh South Cross
Plate 107:   Graiguenamanagh North Cross, west face
Plate 108:   Graiguenamanagh North Cross, east face
Plate 109:   Inishkeel Cross - shaft
Plate 110:   Kilnaboy Tau Cross
Plate 111:   Kells – Cross of Patrick and Columba, north face
Plate 112:   Kells – Cross of Patrick and Columba, west face
Plate 113:   Kells – Cross of Patrick and Columba, south face
Plate 114:   Kells – Cross of Patrick and Columba, east face
Plate 115:   Kells Broken Cross, north face
Plate 116:   Kells Broken Cross, west face
Plate 117:   Kells Broken Cross, south face

IRISH HIGH CROSSES

Plate 118: Kells Broken Cross, east face
Plate 119: Kells Market Cross, north face
Plate 120: Kells Market Cross, west face
Plate 121: Kells Market Cross, south face
Plate 122: Kells Market Cross, east face
Plate 123: Kells Unfinished Cross, east face
Plate 124: Kells Unfinished Cross, west face
Plate 125: Kilbroney Face-cross
Plate 126: Kilbroney Cross, west face
Plate 127: Durrow Cross-head
Plate 128: Lorrha, Cross-base
Plate 129: Kinnitty Cross, north face
Plate 130: Kinnitty Cross, west face
Plate 131: Kinnitty Cross, south face
Plate 132: Doorty Cross, Kilfenora, west face
Plate 133: Doorty Cross, Kilfenora, south face
Plate 134: Doorty Cross, Kilfenora, east face
Plate 135: Kilfenora, cross in field, west face
Plate 136: Kilfenora, cross in field, east face
Plate 137: Kilkieran Plain Cross
Plate 138: Kilkieran Tall Cross, from north-west
Plate 139: Kilkieran Tall Cross, west face
Plate 140: Kilkieran Decorated Cross, north face
Plate 141: Kilkieran Decorated Cross, west face
Plate 142: Kilkieran Decorated Cross, south face
Plate 143: Kilkieran Decorated Cross, base from north-east
Plate 144: Kilkieran Fragments, east face
Plate 145: Kilkieran Fragments, west face
Plate 146: Killamery Cross, north face
Plate 147: Killamery Cross, west face
Plate 148: Killamery Cross, south face
Plate 149: Killamery Cross, east face
Plate 150: Killary Cross, east face
Plate 151: Killary Cross, from north-east
Plate 152: Killary Cross, west face
Plate 153: Kilree Cross, east face
Plate 154: Kilree Cross, west face
Plate 155: Mona Incha Cross
Plate 156: Cross of Muiredach, Monasterboice, north face
Plate 157: Cross of Muiredach, Monasterboice, west face
Plate 158: Cross of Muiredach, Monasterboice, south face
Plate 159: Cross of Muiredach, Monasterboice, east face
Plate 160: Tall Cross, Monasterboice, west face
Plate 161: Tall Cross, Monasterboice, south face
Plate 162: Tall Cross, Monasterboice, east face
Plate 163: North Cross, Monasterboice, west face
Plate 164: Cross of Moone, east face
Plate 165: Cross of Moone, south face
Plate 166: Cross of Moone, west face
Plate 167: Cross of Moone, north face
Plate 168: Old Kilcullen, north face
Plate 169: Old Kilcullen, west face
Plate 170: Old Kilcullen, south face
Plate 171: Old Kilcullen, east face
Plate 172: Onaght, Temple Brecan, shaft of cross
Plate 173: Onaght, Temple Brecan, shaft of cross
Plate 174: Roscrea Cross, east face
Plate 175: Roscrea Cross, west face
Plate 176: St Mullins Cross, east face
Plate 177: St Mullins Cross, west face
Plate 178: Seir Kieran, base, north face
Plate 179: Seir Kieran, base
Plate 180: Termonfeckin Cross, from south

Plate 181: Termonfeckin Cross, from north-west
Plate 182: Termonfeckin Cross, west face
Plate 183: Termonfeckin Cross, east face
Plate 184: Tibberaghny Stone Pillar, north face
Plate 185: Tibberaghny Stone Pillar, west face
Plate 186: Tibberaghny Stone Pillar, south face
Plate 187: Tibberaghny Stone Pillar, east face
Plate 188: Tihilly Cross, north face
Plate 189: Tihilly Cross, west face
Plate 190: Tihilly Cross, south face
Plate 191: Tihilly Cross, east face
Plate 192: Tuam Market Cross, north face
Plate 193: Tuam Market Cross, west face
Plate 194: Tuam Market Cross, south face
Plate 195: Tuam Market Cross, east face
Plate 196: Templeneiry, view of sanctuary about 1909 by H.S. Crawford
Plate 197: Templeneiry Cross-head
Plate 198: Ullard Cross, east face
Plate 199: Ullard Cross, west face

Plate 1:   North Cross, Ahenny, east face

Plate 2:   North Cross, Ahenny, south face

Plate 3:   North Cross, Ahenny, west face

Plate 4:   North Cross, Ahenny, south base

Plate 5:   North Cross, Ahenny north shaft

Plate 6:   North Cross, Ahenny north base

57

Plate 8: The 'Market' Cross, Armagh, cross-head

Plate 7: The 'Market' Cross, Armagh, east face

Plate 9: The 'Market' Cross, Armagh, detail of north face (St Paul and St Anthony)

58

Plate 10: South Cross, Ahenny, north face

Plate 11: South Cross, Ahenny, west face

Plate 12: South Cross, Ahenny, south face

Plate 13: South Cross, Ahenny, east face

Plate 14:   Arboe Cross, west face

Plate 15:   Arboe, south shaft

Plate 16: Arboe, east face of crosshead

Plate 20: Arboe, detail of east face (The Three Children in the Fiery Furnace)

Plate 21: Arboe, detail of south face

Plate 19: Arboe, detail of east face (Daniel in the Lions' Den)

Plate 18: Arboe, detail of east face (Sacrifice of Isaac)

Plate 22: Arboe, detail of north face

Plate 17: Arboe, detail of east face (Adam and Eve)

Plate 23: Bealin Cross, north face   *Plate 24:* Bealin Cross, west face

Plate 25: Bealin Cross, south face

Plate 26: Bealin Cross, east face

Plate 27:   Boho Cross, detail of shaft showing the Fall of Man   *Plate 28:*   Carndonagh, Cross, and pillars, east face

65

Plate 29: Carndonagh, north pillar from west

Plate 30: Carndonagh, south pillar from west

Plate 31: Carndonagh Cross, from south-west

Plate 32: Carndonagh Cross-pillar, east face

Plate 33: Carndonagh Cross-pillar, west face

Plate 34:   St Patrick's Cross, Cashel, east face

68

Plate 36: Castledermot North Cross, east face

Plate 35: Castledermot North Cross, base, north side

Plate 37: Castledermot North Cross, south face

Plate 38: Casltedermot North Cross, west face

70

Plate 39: Castledermot South Cross, north face

Plate 40: Castledermot South Cross, west face

Plate 41: Castledermot South Cross, south face

Plate 42: Castledermot South Cross, east face

72

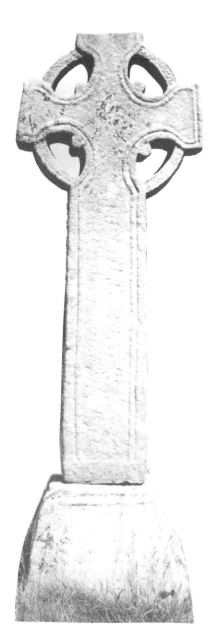

Plate 43: Castlekieran North Cross

Plate 44: Shaft of cross, Banagher Cross, *v.* Clonmacnois

Plate 45: South Cross, Clogher, from east

Plate 46: North Cross, Clogher, from east

74

Plate 47: Clogher Sun-dial, west face

Plate 48: Clogher Sun-dial, east face

Plate 49: Clonca Cross, west face

Plate 50: Clonca Cross, east face

Plate 51: Clones Cross, north face

Plate 52: Clones Cross, east face

Plate 53: Clones Cross, south face

Plate 54: Clones Cross, west face

Plate 55: Clonmacnois North Cross, north face

Plate 56: Clonmacnois North Cross, west face

79

Plate 57: Clonmacnois North Cross, south face

Plate 58: Clonmacnois West Cross

80

Plate 59: Clonmacnois South Cross, north face

Plate 60: Clonmacnois South Cross, west face

Plate 61: Clonmacnois South Cross, south face

Plate 62: Clonmacnois South Cross, east face

Plate 63: Clonmacnois, Cross of the Scriptures, north face

Plate 64: Clonmacnois, Cross of the Scriptures, west face

Plate 65:   Clonmacnois, Cross of the Scriptures, south face

Plate 66:   Clonmacnois, Cross of the Scriptures, east face

84

Plate 67: Donaghmore Cross (Co. Down), west face

Plate 68: Donaghmore Cross (Co. Down), detail of west face

Plate 69: Downpatrick Cross, west face

Plate 70: Downpatrick Cross, east face

Plate 71:   Donaghmore Cross (Co. Tyrone), east face

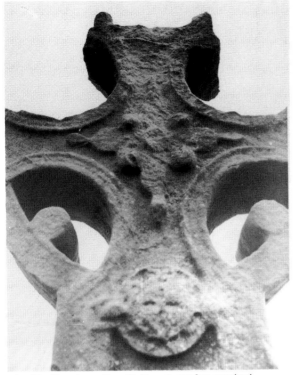

Plate 72: Donaghmore Cross (Co. Tyrone), west face, cross head

Plate 75: Donaghmore Cross (Co. Tyrone),
          detail of west face, (Sacrifice of Isaac)

Plate 74: Donaghmore Cross (Co. Tyrone),
          detail of west face, (Cain and Abel)

Plate 76: Donaghmore Cross (Co. Tyrone), south face, lower half

Plate 73: Donaghmore Cross (Co. Tyrone),
          detail of west face, (Fall of Man)

88

Plate 77: Drumcliff Cross, north face

Plate 78: Drumcliff Cross, west face

Plate 79: Drumcliff Cross, south face   *Plate 80:* Drumcliff Cross, east face

Plate 81:   Duleek Cross, north face   *Plate 82:*   Duleek Cross, west face

Plate 83: Duleek Cross, south face

Plate 84: Duleek Cross, east face

Plate 85: Durrow Cross, north face

Plate 86: Durrow Cross, west face

Plate 87:   Durrow Cross, south face

Plate 88:   Durrow Cross, east face

Plate 89: Dysert O'Dea Cross, north face

Plate 90: Dysert O'Dea Cross, west face

Plate 91: Dysert O'Dea Cross, south face

Plate 92: Dysert O'Dea Cross, east face

Plate 93:   Fahan Mura, Cross-slab, west face

97

Plate 94:   Fahan Mura, Cross-slab, east face

Plate 95:   Fahan Mura, Greek inscription

Plate 96:   Gallen Priory, detail of cross-slab

Plate 97:   Gallen Priory, cross-slab

99

Plate 98: Gallen Priory, grave-slab with ringed cross

Plate 100: Galloon West Cross, head

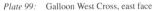

Plate 99: Galloon West Cross, east face

Plate 101: Galloon East Cross, west face

Plate 102: Glendalough 'Market' Cross, west face

Plate 103: Glendalough 'Market' Cross, east face

Plate 104: Dromiskin Cross-head, east face

Plate 105: Dromiskin Cross-head, west face

Plate 106: Graiguenamanagh South Cross

Plate 107: Graiguenamanagh North Cross, west face

Plate 108: Graiguenamanagh North Cross, east face

104

Plate 109: Inishkeel Cross - shaft

Plate 110: Kilnaboy Tau Cross

Plate 111: Kells – Cross of Patrick and Columba, north face   *Plate 112:* Kells – Cross of Patrick and Columba, west face

Plate 113: Kells – Cross of Patrick and Columba, south face

Plate 114: Kells – Cross of Patrick and Columba, east face

108

Plate 115: Kells Broken Cross, north face

Plate 116: Kells Broken Cross, west face

Plate 117: Kells Broken Cross, south face

Plate 118: Kells Broken Cross, east face

110

Plate 119: Kells Market Cross, north face

Plate 120: Kells Market Cross, west face

Plate 121: Kells Market Cross, south face

Plate 122: Kells Market Cross, east face

112

Plate 123: Kells Unfinished Cross, east face

Plate 124: Kells Unfinished Cross, west face

Plate 125: Kilbroney Face-cross

Plate 126: Kilbroney Cross, west face

114

Plate 127: Durrow Cross-head

Plate 128: Lorrha, Cross-base

Plate 130: Kinnitty Cross, west face

Plate 131: Kinnitty Cross, south face

Plate 129: Kinnitty Cross, north face

Plate 132: Doorty Cross, Kilfenora, west face   *Plate 133:* Doorty Cross, Kilfenora, south face   *Plate 134:* Doorty Cross, Kilfenora, east face

Plate 135: Kilfenora, cross in field, west face

Plate 136: Kilfenora, cross in field, east face

Plate 137: Kilkieran Plain Cross   *Plate 138:* Kilkieran Tall Cross, from north-west

Plate 139: Kilkieran Tall Cross, west face

Plate 140: Kilkieran Decorated Cross, north face

120

Plate 141: Kilkieran Decorated Cross, west face

Plate 142: Kilkieran Decorated Cross, south face

121

Plate 143: Kilkieran Decorated Cross, base from north-east

Plate 144: Kilkieran Fragments, east face   *Plate 145:* Kilkieran Fragments, west face

Plate 146: Killamery Cross, north face

Plate 147: Killamery Cross, west face

Plate 148: Killamery Cross, south face

Plate 149: Killamery Cross, east face

124

Plate 151: Killary Cross, from north-east

Plate 150: Killary Cross, east face

125

Plate 152: Killary Cross, west face

Plate 153: Kilree Cross, east face

Plate 154: Kilree Cross, west face

Plate 155: Mona Incha Cross

Plate 156: Cross of Muiredach, Monasterboice, north face

Plate 157: Cross of Muiredach, Monasterboice, west face

Plate 158: Cross of Muiredach, Monasterboice, south face

Plate 159: Cross of Muiredach, Monasterboice, east face

130

Plate 160: Tall Cross, Monasterboice, west face

Plate 161: Tall Cross, Monasterboice, south face

Plate 162: Tall Cross, Monasterboice. east face

Plate 163: North Cross, Monasterboice, west face

Plate 164: Cross of Moone, east face

Plate 165: Cross of Moone, south face

Plate 166: Cross of Moone, west face

Plate 167: Cross of Moone, north face

Plate 168: Old Kilcullen, north face   *Plate 169:* Old Kilcullen, west face

Plate 170: Old Kilcullen, south face   *Plate 171:* Old Kilcullen, east face

Plate 172: Onaght, Temple Brecan, shaft of cross

Plate 173: Onaght, Temple Brecan, shaft of cross

Plate 174: Roscrea Cross, east face

Plate 175: Roscrea Cross, west face

138

Plate 177: St Mullins Cross, west face

Plate 176: St Mullins Cross, east face

Plate 178: Seir Kieran, base, north face

Plate 179: Seir Kieran, base

Plate 180: Termonfeckin Cross, from south

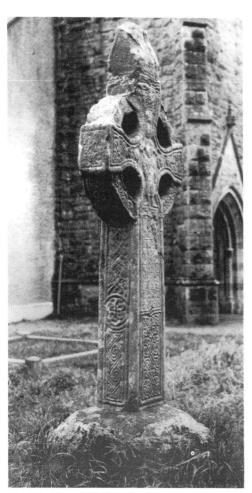

Plate 181: Termonfeckin Cross, from north-west

Plate 182: Termonfeckin Cross, west face

Plate 183: Termonfeckin Cross, east face

142

Plate 184: Tibberaghny Stone Pillar, north face

Plate 185: Tibberaghny Stone Pillar, west face

Plate 186: Tibberaghny Stone Pillar, south face   *Plate 187:* Tibberaghny Stone Pillar, east face

Plate 188: Tihilly Cross, north face

Plate 189: Tihilly Cross, west face

Plate 190: Tihilly Cross, south face

Plate 191: Tihilly Cross, east face

146

Plate 192: Tuam Market Cross, north face

Plate 193: Tuam Market Cross, west face

Plate 194: Tuam Market Cross, south face

Plate 195: Tuam Market Cross, east face

148

Plate 196: Templeneiry, view of sanctuary about 1909 by H.S. Crawford

Plate 197: Templeneiry Cross-head

Plate 198: Ullard Cross, east face

Plate 199: Ullard Cross, west face

Bibliography

General Works

Brandt-Förster, B., *Das Irische Hochkreuz: Ursprung, Entwicklung, Gestalt*, Stuttgart 1978.

Crawford, H.S., 'A Descriptive List of Irish Crosses', *JRSAI* 1907, 187–239; also 1908, 181–2; 1918, pp. 174–9.

Crawford, H.S., *Handbook of Carved Ornament from Irish Monuments of the Christian Period*, Dublin 1926. Reprinted as *Irish Carved Ornament*, Cork 1980.

Flower, R., 'Irish High Crosses', *Journal of the Warburg and Courtauld Institutes*, 1954, pp. 87-97.

Henry, F., *Irish High Crosses*, Dublin 1964.

Lionard, P., 'Early Irish Grave Slabs', *PRIA*, 61C 5, 1961, pp. 95–169.

Ó Murchadha, D., 'Stone Sculpture in Pre-Norman Ireland', *Capuchin Annual*, 1969, pp. 172–200.

Porter, A. Kingsley, *The Crosses and Culture of Ireland*, New Haven 1931.

Roe, H. M., 'The Irish High Cross: Morphology and Iconography', *JRSAI* 1965, pp. 213–226.

Seaborne, M., *Celtic Crosses*, Aylesbury 1989.

Sexton, E.H.L., *Irish Figure Sculpture of the Early Christian Period*, Portland, Maine, 1946.

Streit, J., *Sun and Cross*, Edinburgh 1984.

Inscriptions: selected references

Henry, F., 'Around an Inscription: The Cross of the Scriptures at Clonmacnois', *JRSAI* 1980, pp. 36–46.

Macalister, R.A.S., *Corpus Inscriptionum Insularum Celticarum*, Vol. 2, Dublin 1949.

Ó Murchadha, D., 'Rubbings taken of the Inscriptions on the Cross of the Scriptures, Clonmacnois', *JRSAI* 1980, pp. 47–51.

Ó Murchadha, D. and Ó Murchú, G., 'Fragmentary Inscriptions from the West Cross at Durrow, the South Cross at Clonmacnois, and the Cross of Kinnitty', *JRSAI* 1988, pp. 53-66.

Collected Studies containing major papers on Irish sculpture

Henry, F., *Studies in Early Christian and Medieval Irish Art, Vol. III, Sculpture and Architecture*, London 1985.

Higgitt, J. ed., *Early Medieval Sculpture in Britain and Ireland*, BAR British Series 152, Oxford 1986.

Ryan, M. ed., *Ireland and Insular Art A.D. 500–1200*, Dublin 1987.

Rynne, E. ed., *North Munster Studies*: Essays in commemoration of Monsignor Michael Moloney, Limerick 1967.

Rynne, E. ed., *Figures from the Past*. Studies on figurative art in Christian Ireland in honour of Helen M. Roe, Dublin 1987.

Whitelock, D., *et. al.* eds., *Ireland in Early Medieval Europe*, Cambridge 1982.

Local or regional studies

Byrne, F.J., 'Note on Old Kilcullen', pp. 127-129, *v*. Rynne 1987.

De Bhaldraithe, E., *The High Crosses of Moone and Castledermot, A Guided Tour*. Bolton Abbey, Moone, n.d.

De Paor, L., 'The Limestone Crosses of Clare and Aran', *JGAHS*, 26, 1956, pp. 53–71.

De Paor, L., 'The High Crosses of Tech Theille (Tihilly), Kinnitty, and Related Sculpture', pp. 131–158, *v*. Rynne 1987.

Edwards, N., 'An Early Group of Crosses from the Kingdom of Ossory', *JRSAI* 1983, pp. 5–46.

Edwards, N., 'The South Cross, Clonmacnois (with an appendix on the incidence of Vine-scroll on Irish sculpture)', pp. 23–36, *v*. Higgitt 1986.

Gilling, F.H., 'Ancient Sculptured Cross-Base at Seir-Kieran, Offaly', *JRSAI* 1937, pp. 294–5.

Hamlin, A., 'Two Cross Heads from County Fermanagh: Killesher and Galloon', *UJA* 43, 1980, pp. 53–58.

Hamlin, A., 'Dignatio diei dominici: an element in the iconography of Irish crosses?', pp. 69–75, *v*. Whitelock 1982.

Hamlin, A., 'Some Northern Sundials and Time-keeping in the Early Irish Church', pp. 29–42, *v*. Rynne 1987.

Harbison, P., 'A Group of Early Christian Carved Stone Monuments in County Donegal', pp. 49–86, *v*. Higgitt 1986.

Henry, F., 'A Cross at Durrow (Offaly)', *JRSAI* 1963, pp. 83-4.

Herity, M., 'The Context and Date of the High Crosses at Dísert Diarmada (Castledermot), Co. Kildare', pp. 111–130, *v*. Rynne 1987.

Hickey, H., *Images of Stone*. Figure Sculpture of the Lough Erne Basin, Fermanagh 1985.

Hicks, C., 'A Clonmacnois Workshop in Stone', *JRSAI* 1980, pp. 5–35.

Higgins, J.G., *The Early Christian Cross slabs, Pillar stones and Related Monuments of County Galway, Ireland*, BAR International series 375, i and ii, Oxford 1987.

Historic Monuments of Northern Ireland, HMSO, Belfast 1983.

Lacy, B., *et al.*, *Archaeological Survey of County Donegal*, Lifford 1983.

Lowry-Corry, D., 'The Sculptured Crosses of Galloon', *JRSAI* 1934, pp. 165–176.

Macalister, R.A.S., *Monasterboice, Co. Louth*, Dundalk 1946.

Ó hÉailidhe, P., 'The Crosses and Slabs at St. Berrihert's Kyle, in the Glen of Aherlow', pp. 102–126, *v*. Rynne 1967.

Roe, H.M., 'Antiquities of the Archdiocese of Armagh – A Photographic survey with Notes on the Monuments', *Seanchas Ardmhacha*, Part I: The High Crosses of Co. Louth, 1954, I : I, pp. 101–114; Part II: The High Crosses of Co. Armagh, 1955, I : 2, pp. 107–114; Part III: The High Crosses of East Tyrone, 1956, II : 2, pp. 79–89.

Roe, H.M., *The High Crosses of Western Ossory*, Kilkenny 1958.

Roe, H.M., *The High Crosses of Kells*, Kells 1966.

Roe, H.M., 'A Stone Cross at Clogher, Co. Tyrone', *JRSAI*, 1960, pp. 191–206.

Roe, H.M., *Monasterboice and its Monuments*, Dundalk 1981.

Royal Commission on the Ancient and Historical Monuments of Scotland, *Argyll: An Inventory of the Monuments*, Vol. 4, *Iona*, Edinburgh 1982.

Rynne, E., 'The Tau-Cross at Killinaboy: Pagan or Christian?', pp. 146–165, *v.* Rynne 1967.

Stevenson, R.B.K., 'The Chronology and Relationships of some Irish and Scottish Crosses', *JRSAI*, 1956, pp. 84–96.

Stokes, M., *The High Crosses of Castledermot and Durrow*, Dublin 1898.

Stokes, M., 'Notes on the High Crosses of Moone, Drumcliff, Termonfechin and Killamery', *Trans. RIA*, 1901, pp. 541–578.

Waddell, J., 'An Archaeological Survey of Temple Brecan, Aran', *JGAHS* 1972–73, pp. 5–27.

Waddell, J., 'An Unpublished High Cross on Aran, County Galway', *JRSAI*, 1981, pp. 29–35.

Other Sources Used

Byrne, F.J., *Irish Kings and High Kings*, London 1973.

Grabar, A., *Les Ampoules de Terre Sainte*, Paris 1958.

Hughes, K. and Hamlin A., *The Modern Traveller to the Early Irish Church*, London 1977.

Meehan, D., *Adamnan's De Locis Sanctis*, Dublin 1958.

Weir, A., *Early Ireland: A Field Guide*, Belfast 1980.

More Interesting Books

IRISH SYMBOLS OF 3500 BC

N. L. Thomas

The riddle of the inscriptions at Newgrange, Knowth and other equally ancient Irish sites in the Boyne valley have been partly deciphered at last.

The inscribed passage mound stones tell of prehistoric man's concept of the world; the flat earth with a hemispherical bowl overhead, the sun and the moon circling round.

The legends and myths of Ireland can be directly related to the stone engravings; certain numbers such as nine, eleven, seventeen, twenty-seven and thirty-three are common to both. These numbers have important symbolic meanings as well as their numerical values.

The oldest calender in the history of mankind is portrayed – sixteen months of 22 or 23 days, four weeks of five days each month, eight annual solar and seasonal events. It has been known for some time that the passages into the Newgrange and Knowth mounds are aligned with sunrise and sunset on the solstitial and equinoctial days each year. They are the cornerstones of the sixteen month calender and the eight annual festival days.

The evidence from 3500 BC to 3200 BC precedes British calender building sites at Mount Pleasant 2600 BC and Stonehenge 2000 BC.

A HANDBOOK OF CELTIC ORNAMENT

JOHN G. MERNE

A complete course in the construction and development of Celtic ornament with over 700 illustrations. *A Handbook of Celtic Ornament* takes basic symbols or ideographs and develops them into a systemised method of construction for most forms of Celtic decoration.

Apart from its value as a drawing textbook this book will be of immense valve to all students of Arts and Crafts. The Merne method for the construction and development of Celtic ornament has not been surpassed and this book is a challenge both to the student and the professtional artist to take part of our tradition and make it their own, to use, to repeat, but most of all to develop.

THE GREAT IRISH FAMINE

EDITED BY CATHAL PÓIRTÉIR

This is the most wide-ranging series of essays ever published on the Great Irish Famine and will prove of lasting interest to the general reader. Leading historians, economists, geographers – from Ireland, Britain and the United States – have assembled the most up-to-date research from a wide spectrum of disciplines, including medicine, folklore and literature, to give the fullest account yet of the background and consequences of the Famine.

The Course of Irish History
Edited by T. W. Moody and F. X. Martin

This book provides a rapid short survey, with geographical introduction, of the whole course of Ireland's history. Based on a series of television programmes, it is designed to be both popular and authoritative, concise but comprehensive, highly selective but balanced and fair-minded, critical but constructive and sympathetic. A distinctive feature is its wealth of illustrations.

The present edition is a revised and enlarged version of the original book. New material has been added, bringing the narrative to the IRA ceasefire of 31 August 1994.

Méiní the Blasket Nurse

Leslie Matson

This is the life story of a remarkable woman, Méiní Dunlevy. Born in Massachusetts of Kerry parents, Méiní was reared in her grandparents' house in Dunquin. When she was nineteen, she eloped with an island widower to the Great Blasket, where she worked as a nurse and midwife for thirty-six years. Returning widowed to Dunquin, she died in 1967, aged 91.

Méiní's story, recorded by the author from her own accounts and those of her friends and relatives in Dunquin, is an evocation of a forceful, spicy personality and a compelling reconstruction of a way of life that has exercised an enduring fascination for readers. *Méiní, the Blasket Nurse* is a worthy successor to *An t-Oileánach* and *Twenty Years a-Growing*.

Letters from the Great Blasket

Eibhlís Ní Shúilleabháin

This selection of *Letters from the Great Blasket,* for the most part written by Eibhlís Ní Shúilleabháin of the island to George Chambers in London, covers a period of over twenty years. Eibhlís married Seán Ó Criomhthain – a son of Tomás Ó Criomhthain, An tOileánach (The Islandman). On her marriage she lived in the same house as the Islandman and nursed him during the last years of his life which are described in the letters. Incidentally, the collection includes what must be an unique specimen of the Islandman's writing in English in the form of a letter expressing his goodwill towards Chambers.

Beginning in 1931 when the island was still a place where one might marry and raise a family (if only for certain exile in America) the letters end in 1951 with the author herself in exile on the mainland and 'the old folk of the island scattering to their graves'. By the time Eibhlís left the Blasket in July 1942 the island school had already closed and the three remaining pupils 'left to run wild with the rabbits'.